JUST
LET 'EM
SELL

JUST
LET 'EM
SELL

STEVEN
HENRY

Library of Congress Control Number:		2008907527
ISBN:	Hardcover	978-1-4363-6332-7
	Softcover	978-1-4363-6331-0

This book was printed in the United States of America.

To order additional copies of this book, contact:
Xlibris Corporation
1-888-795-4274
www.Xlibris.com
Orders@Xlibris.com
50676

Contents

Opening Pitch

When my salespeople would come to see or call me, there would always be the conversation of a customer order they just received or lost. That is what selling is—winning and losing, not much in between. I would often coach them that the biggest challenge they had was to keep an even keel or they will never learn how to be happy in the sales profession. It is okay to celebrate a win and likewise mourn a loss. Just keep it in perspective, and do not dwell on either too long.

I could go into much more as to a day in a salesperson's life. It is one made up of so many emotional ups and downs many people wonder why anyone would even choose the selling profession. Salespeople have to live on the road, have no real chance to vent at the coffee machine with other inner company employees, and then must be fairly pleasant to everyone, sometimes for eighteen hours a day. So why would anyone want this to be a job for life? I know why, and I did it in corporate life for twenty years while still doing it today in my own business. We salespeople thrive on ongoing daily challenges!

So this book is about sales teams and their supporting company cast. I write this book more from the manufacturer's perspective as that is where I spent my career in selling. Does this mean the information in this book will only work for manufacturing companies? The answer is no; anyone can apply the practices and disciplines discussed in this book. I make an effort to show how any company that has a sales team can use the information and suggestions. I used these techniques with my teams to grow sales revenue year over year. I go into some very basic discussion about what makes a successful sales team and how to apply some simple tools to accomplish this. I found over my career that companies continue to try and complicate the sales process. For this reason, I will go to great extremes to point out how to simplify the sales process. Through many new customers-planning techniques, along with numerous other management-controlling programs, it is no wonder many salespeople I have talked to over the years are just plain frustrated and confused. With all these obstacles in the way, it is easy to understand why the salespeople in many of these companies have much less time to "just sell."

If you are really sincere about letting your sales team grow sales revenue, then you must simplify the duties that block your sales team from getting orders. Stop trying to control this bunch of mustangs and let them run. Your sales team is different than any other group you have in the company so manage them like they are.

By following just a few suggestions from this book, you will find improved sales revenues, less turnover from the top salespeople, a more positive interaction with your customers, and a sales team that is viewed as very professional in their industry. I have tried to lay out the chapters to flow as if you were to start up a whole new sales program. Conversely if you are just interested in, let's say, creative compensation packages for your sales team, then you could focus on that chapter only.

Well, so much for my "pitch." Enjoy the reading and quit making this so difficult; all a sales team wants their company to do is "just let 'em sell"!

Maximizing their teams sales time along with positive motivation is one of the most important parts of a sales leader's responsibilities.

Chapter 1

Take Away the Barriers of Getting Orders

I arrived in my new VP-of-sales job right on time Monday morning. I was introduced to a few people and then taken to my office. After getting a few more visitors, it was up to me to start looking through piles of papers which were to orient me to the company. This went on for the day and I left with a head full of information and more questions. In the forthcoming days, I continued my orientation process which generated questions and it was time to start getting answers to those questions. One thing that struck me was a large stack of computer printouts that were on my desk each morning. Each Monday I had a six-inch stack of reports waiting on my desk when I arrived and was informed that these were from the sales team. The reports consisted of activities from each salesperson from the previous week. They were very detailed and many managers of the company received them each week.

Getting back to the stack of computer printouts with numbers, it would take hours to look over if one was serious about looking at them. I talked to some of my sales directors and asked them about the weekly sales activity report. A few said it was necessary in order to find out what their team was doing. A few others said it took time from the sales process as salespeople usually spend at least a half day to get it prepared and sent in. I then started to ask about the need for these weekly reports and the daily computer reports. You would have thought I committed murder! I was more or less told that the computer reports were read by each manager every day and the weekly reports were reviewed by many more than just the top management. I was now in my third week and thought it might be a good time to really find out what this is all about. My instructions were to stop the daily pack of sales result printouts and also to tell the sales team to stop the weekly report and just go sell. I told the computer people to give a summary report out to all management daily on a few simple sheets showing the highlights of the orders the previous day and that is all. I was told by a few people that this would not be acceptable and I had better be prepared to get called into the boss's office and explain why I did this.

Well, one day went by, then two, then a week. No calls from anyone. I then began to ask the management team how they liked the summary report. It was unanimous—it was easy to review and understand and it also gave them a snapshot of how business was doing. I received no requests for the weekly sales report. What was happening? Well, it was simple: everyone was very busy running their own internal business, and they had limited time to review the numbers in detail. It was the same with the sales report. These managers were working long hours with their teams and did not have the time to review a sales team report, which is the same with me as I would not have time to read about activities of all other departments. If revenues were coming in, then that was good enough for the company management team.

I also never liked attending the numerous meetings that were held to discuss where the company was headed. I was open to a meeting like this once a month; at that time we could review where the sales team was as to meeting their goals. I always thought it was an opportunity to make excuses as to why someone or some team was falling short of their commitments. I was always willing to attend a meeting to set goals over an agreed-upon period of time. What was never acceptable to me was when managers agreed upon what they and their team would accomplish only to fall short of their commitments then come to the next meeting with excuses and be allowed to set another commitment. A sales management team must take full responsibility to meet the assignment given to them and assure company management that their team will perform. Many times management does not allow a team to perform. They set a route then jerk to another and another in short periods of time. They also load up the teams with too much paperwork and reports so people cannot focus on getting things done. In this book, I will focus on the sales team aspect even though I am sure these ideas can be used company-wide. My main message is that people must be left alone to perform, and that is what I will discuss in detail throughout this book.

I have no time for revisiting what I commit to, and I believe that companies should do less reasoning as to why something did not get done and focus more on getting it done. Sales teams should not be burdened with anything that prevents them from getting the orders their company needs to meet their plans. This is easy to say, but I fought many battles to convince and make sure the people in different levels of the company remembered what the sales team's responsibilities were. If you are with a company doing this, then this book is for you. Why are so many reports needed when these affect the productivity of a company? It seems that departments outside of sales are very curious as to how sales teams function. What some want to do is monitor and see the sales team managed similar to the other internal company groups. What has been proven over and over is that when you do this, the results are lower sales revenue, higher sales team turnover from usually the best players, wasted productive time, and customer anxiety.

There was once a senior manager in a company who asked "what makes a good salesperson." A good example is a sales person who spends all day preparing for a sales presentation. They call on the customer with their presentation and as they begin their well-prepared presentation, the customer asks a question totally unrelated and wants to only talk about his subject. A truly great salesperson closes his computer and talks the rest of the time on the customer issue saving his presentation for another time. The senior manager who asked this question then said, "It sounds as if a good salesperson has a major genetic defect."

This is true. The example at the start of this chapter regarding weekly detailed reports is one way to slow a sales team down. When we informed the sales team that they did not have to spend their day on getting the weekly report ready and they could go out and sell, I was challenged by a few salespeople who wanted to do the report for the management team. As you probably guessed, I reviewed their sales results and all the challengers were on the bottom of the list. Conversely top performers were elated as now they had more time to sell. Salespeople who are top performers will welcome less reporting especially if those reports bring the sales process little, if any, value. For a salesperson, it is critical to have time to learn products, prepare for product promotions, and schedule his time effectively. They are many times burdened and must deal with customer and channel calls that relate way too often to after-sales situations. The company must strive to have their sales teams spend a large part of their time on presale preparations and obtaining orders. This is why a consistent and simple review of what the sales team is doing and why should be a company's top priority. A sales team should be held responsible for keeping the company healthy. They are responsible for keeping the company's employees employed. This may sound a bit dramatic, but think about it for a while. Any company I was ever associated with went through good times and bad. I remember the horrible feeling I had when I had to go to a company meeting to discuss why the orders were slowing down. When the explanation was over, the meeting agenda went directly to a discussion on how the company could bring costs into line in order to "save the quarter." I knew what this meant, and it was employee cutbacks. Anyone who has managed budgets knows the one real way to reduce the costs is to eliminate people. This is a very grim but true view of how companies are run. I constantly emphasized to my sales teams the importance of getting orders for the good of all company employees and their families.

If you were to start a company today, the sales team would have to focus immediately on the basics of preparation. In order to sell, they would have to start a customer management program. They would need customer information, contacts, and a strategy to call on this customer. They would then have to make contact and keep notes ongoing as to what happens with this customer over time. Thankfully, this is something all companies have if they have been in business over time. This information can be an in-house/individually designed customer management program or one of the many available from third-party companies in the market today. I will not contest the need for this even though I will challenge the extent of how much information one needs to be successful in selling to a chosen customer. Now, if a salesperson is responsible for one large customer, then his customer management program will most probably be extensive as these are normally complicated selling environments. I will show, though, how you can still simplify even this situation so as to focus on what is really going on at any given time in the order process.

Every salesperson must be released to sell, sell, sell. They should wake up at night with only one thing on their mind and that is where their next order will come from tomorrow. The problem I have seen over time is that the salespeople are being pushed toward acting and performing like other company departments. No department can be treated like another because they all have all different types of personalities and duties that are different. The sales teams must be challenged and totally focused on bringing in orders for the company. A saying we used many times was the fact that "more sales cure what ails." This is easy to understand as a strong order-focused sales team can make a huge impact on the whole company. I have never seen a company who has too many orders conduct meetings on reducing anything except lead times.

I went as far to tell my sales teams that they did not have to do any new reporting unless it was approved by me and my management team. It is very easy for someone in the company to request something from a salesperson, and many times that person will just do it so as not to cause conflict. The sales team must be educated and disciplined to understand that their most important job is to get orders, not to fill out forms that prevent them from bringing in sales revenues. Well, enough philosophy; let's get into the meat of reporting and what I have found to be very effective.

So what types of reports are needed, and how do you get buy-in from other departments within your company as to their effectiveness? When my team had the best sales results, we also had the least reports. This was both in good and difficult times in regard to sales revenue results. The challenge is when times are bad, everyone in corporations want micromanagement imposed on all. My belief is that when times are tough, you open the floodgates and attack with focus and basic sales tactics. So reports need to be simple, easy to review, and easy to fill out. My choice over the years was an Excel type sheet listing all the items that are really important to getting orders. I want to emphasize "important to getting orders" so that the sheet does not fill up with useless information.

Our best results were when we asked other departments to assist us in putting sales planning sheets together. Set some simple rules with the most important being any item listed that must be related to getting orders. You must keep constant vigil on this one as over time, someone will try to start adding things that they believe need to be known only to find out it has nothing to do with helping get the order. You will see a sample sheet (item 1a) in which I have just picked out a few items that focus on orders that the particular salesperson is pursuing.

Let's review some suggested items that are important when it comes to getting orders. Please stop here and understand what I just said again: "important to getting orders." Again, remember the many times companies request the sales team to fill out detailed reports on customers and opportunities while forgetting what is really needed to get an order. Sales management can be talked into reporting massive amounts of information that never gets reviewed and it is a waste of time for everyone. So what is important? Let's look at a few items:

- Customer name—Duh?
- What products are they buying now? This is helpful because if your company manufactures ten product lines and the existing customer is buying five, then there is an opportunity to grow business through someone that buys from you today. In my experience, this is overlooked time after time.
- What is the current sales opportunity in product and revenue?
- Where are we in the sales cycle? Now, some companies like the percentage rule. That is, what the salesperson's view of the percentage of getting the order is. Then the finance people use this percent to forecast revenue. I will review an example of this after I list a few more items.
- What is the immediate sales situation or need?
- What date is the next customer meeting?
- What help do you need to get to the next step?
- When do you anticipate the decision, the end date?

Let's take a look at a simple spreadsheet with the needed information to allow someone to make decisions on the current sales opportunities.

SHEET (1a)

Oppor-tunity	Customer Name	$ Amount	Sales-person	Current products used	Stage of sales process	Annual sales revenue forecast	Needs to help close deal	Current actions	Order placed	End date
Product 1	Acme A	100K	T Jones	A,C	3	500K	New proposal	Working on date to deliver next week	N	7-1
Product 2	Acme 2	250K	B. Keel	B	4	50K	Management visit	Next Monday meeting	N	6-29
Product 3	Acme 3	50K	H. Stevens	None	5	0	Got order		Y	6-15
Product 4	Acme 4	200K	T. Jones	B	2	300K	Review pricing	Conference call schedules 3pm on the 5th	N	7-5
Product 5	Acme 5	150K	B. Keel	A,B,C	1	500K	Initial presentation	Working proposal with mktg	N	7-12
Product 6	Acme 6	25K	M. Grant	C	3	200K	Meet purchasing	Schedule meeting for next week	N	7-1
Product 7	Acme 7	35K	T Jones	None	3	0	Factory visit	Setting date for visit	N	7-20

I suggest you have your IT people create this sheet and allow people to sort cells that are important. You could look at a product group to see what type of activity there is. You also might want to find out how many opportunities a particular salesperson is working on or what the revenue total is for all current next thirty-day projects. This type of sorting keeps it simple; and by keeping these sheets current, it will decrease the workload on the sales, finance, and marketing teams when they go looking for information from the field. A good example is when the finance team needs to attend a quick management meeting to report on order forecast for the next two weeks. They can take core everyday order rates from the computer and then access this sheet to sort the next two weeks of forecasted orders. This will give the core orders forecast from history or run rate along with the larger order forecast the sales team is focused on to close.

The previous sheet contains sales process items we have used in the past for my own sales territory and with my team. They can be anything you choose; the main thing to remember is not to overload the sheet with things that do not assist in getting the order. There is a tendency to add items that just fill up the sheet and make it very complicated to use effectively. Some areas of explanation might be needed for the columns of current products used and stage of sales process. Current products could be grouped in any way you see fit. The idea is just to get a quick understanding of what, if any, products you offer are being used by this particular customer. Of course, the more of your products they are currently using then the better you will have a feeling as to the chances of getting the order for your current opportunity. One other benefit of this is that if a selected customer is using a majority of your products but not moving forward with one on the sheet, you have an excellent way to get feedback on why they are delaying a decision.

The "stages of a sales process" is critical in order to keep moving in some direction whether it be forward or removal from the sheet. Many times a sales opportunity will stall and if not targeted quickly will just lie there and stagnate. In a complicated reporting process, it is difficult to target these and a few excuses can just move them into a limbo stage. I will discuss this further in the chapter on customers as you must not get trapped into the customer-excuse whirlpool. With this simple and effective spreadsheet, you force the situation to move forward or remove it from the sheet. Every salesperson must have a customer and territory strategies as this is what continually feeds this spreadsheet. A customer strategy is a high-level view of how a salesperson will penetrate a customer with as many products as possible being offered by their company. Many times this becomes a very detailed review and is done in many different ways. Implementing a simple sheet like this is a way to break through all the details so they do not complicate the current opportunities. You may be thinking that this simple breakdown spreadsheet will not drive performance.

I have found exactly the opposite. As stated, every salesperson must have a customer plan in place ongoing and updated frequently. The problem with a detailed plan is judging performance. When there is too much to focus on at one time, then it is impossible to follow just what is happening at any given time. With the simple spreadsheet I have found, it is a great way to take their details and break them into focused measurable pieces. I discuss performance measurements later in the book and I will continue to try to convince doubters that this process absolutely demands winning performance. One last thing is that when implementing this spreadsheet strategy, you will find who the sub par salespeople are, and it will become evident quickly. The ones who used the details of a complicated plan to escape meeting their sales revenue goals become very visible. I have also found that it is these exact salespeople who do not like this program as it demands positive performance. Do not fear as the other good news is they normally leave on their own before you have to take action. Salespeople who make excuses on why they are falling short of getting orders will not be able to work under these conditions. Top performers will excel as they now have the company resources targeting their projects, which is very powerful in growing their territory revenues.

Now, back to the selling process on how to judge and evaluate the current situation. The sales process needs to be defined by your company. One way I have seen many companies do this is by old "percent of order status." The "percent of order status" is something that drove me nuts. This also is one very direct example of the salesperson's mind compared to people who have never been a true salesperson. When others want to know the percentage of a sale, they then want to try and apply this to sales revenue. So if the percent of getting a $100k order is 50 percent, then we will put down $50k on the sheet. This is what drove me crazy as it had nothing to do with revenue, but it happens over and over at company meetings. What we did was to break down the process to fit your "needs to know" for any listed sales opportunity. Break it down to percent increments and drive the cycle to move forward. A typical set of increments could be the following:

- Find the opportunity—10 percent
- Propose a solution—10 percent

- Feedback on the solution—10 percent
- Make sure you have decision makers at the customer on board—20 percent
- Make a proposal and get buy-in from the decision-making team—20 percent
- List any items/actions we need to obtain the order—20 percent
- Close the order—10 percent

Take these and assign numbers that are easy to apply to the sheet so that everyone knows quickly where you are at with this opportunity. When the number does not change over a defined period turn the red light on and decide what to do. This is what again makes this so simple. Define the increments, list them, and follow them up with passion. Remember, this sheet is made to push the process to closure be it an order or off the sheet and to go after another opportunity.

Let's look at an example of how this might be used on a particular order opportunity. If we use the criteria from the previous list and we are at 50 percent, then this would mean we are at the decision-making stage. Now, anyone involved can then ask logical questions as to what we need to do to help get the decision go our way. The real issue is that an order is a 100 percent and we need to keep the process moving in that direction. It is not an order at any given time before we get the customer commitment, and it is the company's responsibility to help the sales team move the process forward to obtain this commitment. This part of the spreadsheet must be reviewed continually by the sales team management and oftentimes weekly by the people responsible to help the salespersons close the order. If an opportunity is sitting in the 40 or 50 percent stage for more than a decided-on time frame, then move it forward or take it off. Only allow the list of opportunities that are moving toward order commitment to stay posted on the sheet. A good sales team always will have multiple opportunities, and it is the responsibility of sales management to discover which ones are the ripest ones to be listed on this sheet. The responsibility of sales management is to drive the sales team to move current real opportunities into revenue while also loading up the next wave.

When managing this type of program, it focuses on the customer and what is needed to make an order happen. This program also keeps the sales team focused and driving forward for orders. In a later chapter, I will discuss how this will also assist the management team in evaluating sales team performance. As this process is implemented, you may see an increase of excuses as to why the process is not moving forward. I will not state the excuses because we have heard them all. What I will suggest is a way to break through excuses and move the process forward. This is fairly simple. Just listen and I mean really listen to the excuse. Once the excuse is stated, just ask what is needed to move this opportunity forward. Now you must stay on the course and not let another excuse take place of the answer to your question. The answer must be some type of action that really gets the process back on track. If it is a mundane of soft-action plan, then stop the conversation and dig in deep to find out what is going on. Do not let the salesperson off the hook without setting a plan to move forward on this quickly, which means right after this phone call or meeting is over. Remember, this is the hot list, not the list of fifty opportunities. This list is the next week or two of company orders, and that is what you need to always stay focused on. All excuses are an opportunity. Here is the summary on how to manage this program to keep it focused and effective:

- Solve the problem and keep moving forward.
- Remove the sales opportunity from the list and go for the next one.
- Challenge a particular salesperson if there is a trend of excuses for which may just lead to weak opportunities on their particular list.
- Define if there is a true product or service deficiency that the company must address.

This last one is a difficult one to deal with from a sales perspective. We had a new product line that the company had spent millions of dollars developing. The release date was delayed, and the market for the product changed before we could really start to promote it. The sales team followed many of the plans to promote and within months was spending too much time on a product line that was destined to be a failure. The customers were not interested, and the product was not right for the market for many reasons. Now, these reasons were viewed as excuses and the company was not going to extend any more money into the product unless the sales team could bring in some orders. The sales team was instructed to keep promoting and get orders. I remember weekly conference calls with upper management detailing each sales opportunity and the inevitable question, "Why can't you get some orders?" No matter what we factually told them, their listening mode was shut off. We beat this product line to death while revenues of other products began to decrease as the sales team was focused on "politically" doing what was right to keep them off the hot seat. The real problem was promotion of a weak product while spending many hours filling our reports on why they could not get the customer to purchase this product.

I tell this story because it happens all the time and to me personally in the past from different product groups. Rather than just letting the sales team get back to selling once it was established these products are not going anywhere, the company management continued to waste precious sales time. This is not to say the sales team should not be challenged; they should be constantly challenged to sell every company product and meet the goals assigned to them. What the other department managers need to realize is when to move forward or regroup a product line. Honestly, look at what is going on, lean back; take a deep breath, look in the mirror. In this case, we wasted valuable sales time, irritated distributors and customers, while falling behind competition with our other product offerings. In fact, I know of a few cases where the competition knew our sales team was focusing on a new promotion so they attacked our other areas and converted customers while we were busy focused on a failed promotion. The saying goes and is used all the time, "If it isn't right, the dog won't eat"; this simple saying is so true.

Another reality is when directing your sales group you must have their faith so they are willing and able to respond to emergencies. By emergencies, I mean sometimes actions have to be taken to help the company meet certain goals. A product line needs one more big push to meet some type of established outcome; the quarter needs a strong last week of orders to meet some shortfalls. These are examples your sales team must embrace; and I found that by creating a sales process that is very focused, your team will, in turn, go the extra mile to turn these types of emergencies into completed successes.

Just a comment on this simplified program and how it can work in any environment. I was assigned to the Asia Pacific region with Rockwell for a period of five years. Working out of your base country is difficult in many ways as anyone who has worked in this type of environment knows too well. I also realized very quickly how important it was to drive the sales review process to the simplest form possible. You must get to the real issue quickly, and I found this true when in Japan at the start of my assignment and even more so when managing the entire region which included ten to twelve countries. The excuses from the sales team and customers on why a product does not fit were numerous when I was in the United States. Internationally, it is mind-boggling and as I started my assignment it was clear why sales revenues were struggling. We decided to make the process easy and try to find out what the real opportunities were and what customers really wanted to work with us. It is important to emphasize "really" as this is the key to any successful customer sales strategy. Many customers are just too nice to flat out tell you they do not want or will not buy your products. The sales management and sales team must dissect the customer base continually so time utilization is maximized. I have seen so much time wasted on pursuing customers or calling on the wrong contact at a customer's when time could and should have been spent on "higher potential for orders" customers. Internationally, I would typically visit our operations in a given company for a week at a time. This is normal as you fly in so why be in a hurry to leave. This gives time for reviews plus visits throughout this time period to selected customers. I also found that when the "boss" arrived, the treatment was first-class. Meetings were very formal, and presentations were fairly lengthy. Of course, there were many questions and, as usual, equal amount of reasons as to why the sales numbers were not meeting plan. I also always had that feeling, as I was flying out at the end of my visit that the in-country people were giving high fives as to all the information they gave me to decipher. They knew it would keep me busy and maybe I would leave them alone until my next visit when they could load me up again. This whole situation is happening even in small regions with any type of sales team; it is just expanded when working a complicated region. You must get the process down to the simplest terms and strive to keep it there. I found this focused spreadsheet worked even in countries with challenges of culture, language, unique product requirements, and all the other challenges a company faces. In fact, it was probably the only way I kept any sanity in a fast-paced confusing environment.

So now you have a simple way to manage your sales team and focus on the main and current opportunities. Now, how do you coach your team to balance time to get the most out of a sales day? I have some simple suggestions that work if they are implemented and personal discipline is applied. Let's look at a few:

1. **Ways to see the customer on a regular basis other than always face-to-face.**

Yes, you must stay in touch with the customer, but why always face-to-face? Customers are very busy and many times are happy to see you when you can help them. Social time is important so schedule it and remember, when going to see a customer on business, then take them something valuable, which could be just good listening skills. Another way to see a customer is to phone or e-mail them on a regular basis. I was amazed at how many times a customer told me he got to know me very well over the phone between sales calls. Customers talk differently and if busy can call you back and usually do. By the way, if they continually do not call you back then you have something to deal with and at least know where you stand. This saves travel time and is very efficient in many other ways. I established a schedule each week not only of who I was going to visit but also who I was going to call on the phone. I did this even in my VP role and it is a great way to build relationships without spending too much time with any given person. I also challenge any salesperson to tell me they do not have enough time to phone a customer. How many minutes does a salesperson listen to the radio in their car? The day is only so long and the opportunities to contact and sell over the phone are right there in you mobile or home office. This also gives you a chance to improve your listening skills and really hear what the customer is saying.

2. Making the home office productive.

If you feel a salesperson is not productive in their home office, then it is one of two things: you have a management problem or you have a weak salesperson. These are the only two reasons. I asked some of my sales team what they would do in their home office when I first started to stay home more often from the corporate office when not traveling. I wanted to figure out a routine when working from home as it was a big change for me. We talked together and over time we started to list ways to make home office time very productive, calling marketing people to discuss strategies, distributors to review their sales plans, customers to set up visits or discuss new promotions. Many times an e-mail with an attachment would be sent so we could review it on the phone. One main concern would always come up: company personnel should be required to schedule time for business review calls when the sales team would be in their home office. I was always amazed at calls that were set up midweek for sales reviews or just plain questions that disrupted the salesperson's time or pulled them out of a customer meeting. Many times these calls came out of the blue and caught the salesperson off guard and then took their mind off what they were currently doing. Many times, they were given hurry-up tasks and then these would disrupt their selling routine. These could have been scheduled a few days later when the salesperson was in their home office. It is not just the salesperson's responsibility to make home office time productive but it is everyone's since the most important time in the week is in the field and should be totally focused on selling. Company management should also take advantage and schedule time with salespeople on the phone when in their home office.

One area that is still underused, even though it is promoted in many discussions, is Web site selling and training. Customers and channels to market are busy, and many welcome a discussion and presentation over the computer and phone. Training this way is a great opportunity that must be in the annual planning for the company. Sales teams should also force themselves to hold a few customer sales presentations weekly from their home office. When I talked to customers about this, they were positive as their day was always full, and this type of interaction offered them a chance to be very effective and efficient with their limited time.

We left the hotel in the morning to call on a customer who we thought would be a good candidate for some of our new products. They were rebuilding their facility, and we had the technology to get them to the next level. This was a team call with the salesperson and me the VP sales. I like team calls as when worked correctly they give time to listen as others talk. Listening is the most important sense to have in sales. We talk and read about it, practice it, and then when in a presentation or meeting, forget all about it. The customer gave us a few minutes to get into the presentation then asked some basic questions. He also told us in a very hidden way what he really needed and that the competition could not provide. As the observer, I changed the game plan to focus on his comments that seemed to be minor in importance but were very key to getting him to buy in on our proposal. This then expanded to a whole new conversation and took us to the next level of the sales process for this opportunity. My point is that many salespeople do not particularly like team calls with others, especially management. This is because many times they get critiqued and challenged after the sales call as to why they did this or that. Rather than listen to the customer, the team observer listens to the sales pitch and the customer reaction. The problem is they do not listen for opportunities and then help the salesperson. Now many will say they do, but I challenge them in saying they do not hear the real opportunity because they are also concentrating on how the salesperson is performing. This is the exact thing we should not do in a sales call. I have even seen some pull out a personal communication unit and read their e-mails!

When I was in Japan, I witnessed and learned for three years what it really meant to listen. I could not speak the language other than basic survival even though I studied the language for the time I was there. So I had to quickly improve my listening skills and understand body language. Aki Suzuki, our president for Japan operations, gave me valuable training in listening, and I was astonished at how well I could follow a meeting and understand what was going on just by listening for the words I knew and watching body movements and facial expressions. I improved these skills to where I needed minimum translation toward the end of my assignment and understood for the first time how powerful listening and watching were in a sales call.

One last area to address is the sales routine. This must change frequently so as to keep a salesperson fresh and motivated. This keeps your job exciting and also encourages a salesperson to devise new ways to approach a customer. Some problems a sales team encounters are company management or third-party companies hired by the management to work with sales teams. These working sessions normally consist of new ways to help the sales team become more productive. Help is many times defined as new ways to sell that includes more reports or improved monitoring programs. I wondered many times if a GPS and alarm collar would be implemented after leaving a few of these "improve sales effectiveness" meetings. These were usually suggested by people who were never in sales and also never took the time to travel with salespeople on a routine basis. What happens with these new plans is they almost always slow down the sales process by burdening the sales team with nonselling activities. The idea is to speed up, simplify, and increase the sales activities. You do this, and you will create efficiencies that will always increase sales numbers. I would suggest what I told many people who came up with these new programs to just take a minute to look at what they are trying to accomplish and then evaluate if this will speed up or slow down a given salesperson. The best programs we came up with were when selected internal company management and sales team members would team up and talk through ideas on how to speed up the sales process to get more orders. The companies I worked for paid me and my team a great amount of money to sell our products and all they had to do is give us direction and let us figure it out. Companies need to do just that and strive not to overcomplicate the process of selling. The selling process is delicate in terms of keeping it a selling process while preventing it from turning into something it was not meant to be. It is a process that unless you do it and become very good at it, you derail and slow it down then it is very hard to get back on track. Changes need to constantly be made for growth; just keep the changes focused around what the selling machine in a company is responsible for, and make sure not to slow it down with programs not applicable at all to this sales process.

We decided one year to increase the size of the expense reports for the entire company. It would be very detailed and reviewed weekly by finance and sales management. The sales team would now be spending more time on detailing exactly what they did each day in regard to spending money, keeping even the smallest receipt and using only one type of credit card and working totally with a travel agent. So a few weeks went by and finance was concerned the sales team was not turning their reports in weekly, and when they did, there was not enough detail. One complaint was that some salespeople even bypassed the travel agent (I by mistake instructed my team to always call the travel agent) and did their own things for hotels and flights at times during the week. They now wanted to have conference calls with selected sales team members who were not "doing it right." This was the real winner for us in sales as no matter how much sales management pleaded with company management not to implement this new expense program in its entirety to the sales team, the more people thought we were hiding something. They did not just sit back and realize we, the sales management, knew this would slow down the sales team from their selling activities. We were not against controlling expenses, but just make it easy and give us the guidelines we needed to follow. So now, back to the first set of calls with the selected sales team. They complained that getting receipts for every little thing was difficult and many times impossible. Some places took one type of credit card; the other did not. The travel agency was not equipped for all the new calls, and being on hold for extended time was common. By the way, the sales team had all the tools needed to set their own reservations (computers) 50 percent of the time or more, so why not let them do it to save time. In fact, they showed proof that they had ways to buy less expensive air tickets and hotel rooms than the travel agency. We were looking for some type of mix that made sense and the real problem is here we were taking up productive sales time discussing expenses during critical selling hours. After a time period of doing this, we went and developed a "mix" focused on speeding up process which was a lesson learned by all.

There is a simple and effective way to assure the sales team is meeting the timelines for reports such as expenses. We also discovered an easy method to get the point across as to the importance of filling out the expense reports accurately and honestly. How did we do this? I would start out a sales meeting and discuss certain subjects. I would make a short but very direct point regarding reports and key on the expense report example. The conversation was that it is the particular salesperson's responsibility to fill the reports out correctly, and if there were questions, then we would help. If they were filled out dishonestly, then they would lose their job, plain and simple! The point is that a company should not have to check reports for honesty or correctness. Once trained, then it is a "no-brainer." Why spend any time on discussing it? Set expectations early on, and you will have minimal problems with the team. By the way, word got out quickly that a person did not want me to be calling them on this issue as it was a very one-sided conversation. I just wanted my team to know that we were supporting them by keeping things simple so they could do their job and go get orders. I also said that there should be no need to check an expense report because the expectation was to fill them out correctly and honestly. You will find it was easy and nonconfrontational.

I have given ideas in this chapter that will achieve the needs of the company in strengthening your sales team and ultimately growing sales. I also hope you will see why it is important to speed up the sales process and think through what you require from your sales team in regard to their accomplishments. The more reports, rules, and nonsales-focused programs you implement, the less sales revenues you will get. So why not just let them sell!

You get what you pay for so create sales team compensation to encourage exceeding individual sales plans year over year

Chapter 2

Compensate for Revenue Growth

One of the best things I did in my younger years was joining the United States Navy right after high school. I became a navy diver, and the discipline given to me by the navy has stayed with me all my life. I learned how to accomplish things that I thought were impossible. The reason I left the service was to get a college degree as I was ready for the corporate world even though life in the military was good and it is a great career. I remember the start of what convinced me I was destined for opportunities that rewarded me for exceeding normal situations. In the military, discipline is a must and following orders without question is critical to survive. I learned this quickly and learned something about people and those that excel and how they compare to others. At port one day, we were told that if we completed all of our tasks in good fashion and finished early, we could then go on early leave when done. Now, I did understand that the normal practice is to complete work in good timing but not too quickly as you want to be always busy. Our leader gave us more than the normal workload so as to make sure we did not get done early. Little did he know, our team was full of achievers ready for a challenge. Well, we completed our tasks three hours early and were ready for inspection and early shore leave. Our leader was a bit surprised and figured the work would be a bit sloppy, only to find out it was all done in acceptable fashion. We could see his nervousness as he told us he would have to check on the early leave and get back to us. We ended up leaving with everyone else at normal time for shore leave. You can imagine our disappointment and then in a few days we again were told that now he had approval to let us go early and gave us our work schedule, which was again a long list. Our team made up their mind to get it done, and we did with time to spare. Our leader approved the work and then informed us we would have to help in an urgent work situation and the early leave would occur in the near future. What is that saying about fool us once, fool us twice?

We never did get the leave nor did we take that bait again, but I got a valuable lesson on achievers and rewards. Now, this story may sound like just a service story, but I saw this same type of thing happen all the time in corporate settings. How many companies today put together a sales compensation program that does not motivate for high growth? Most people think they have one, but they do not. Salespeople know from the start of each year what the company revenue goal is and how their individual plans add up to equal the company plans. Most sales compensation plans miss the opportunity to encourage their sales teams to beat their own plans. The salespeople know when they meet their goals and if there is no expanded compensation plan for them then they have no motivation to exceed these planned goals. For example, by beating their plan, they then know in the following years they will be challenged to grow even more and this could negatively affect their compensation and performance review. Unless you really give them a big win opportunity when they beat their assigned goal, then you face the reality of things slowing down once they obtain their numbers. Why would this be? A few ideas are as follows:

- Their commission does not increase on additional sales over plan, so why put in that extra effort for the same dollars when you have made a pretty good income and it is late in the year.
- If I sell more this year than I was assigned, then my number goes way up next year and will reduce if I don't.
- If we do sell more and take the company over plan, they get a big benefit while we just get the same rate of commission and sometimes less. This is where the breakdown of loyalty and aggressiveness begins to occur.

You might be thinking this never happens in your company, and if you do, then you are not facing reality. A great sales compensation plan challenges your sales team not only to meet but exceed the company sales plans. I am writing this book to give you some insight as to what the people in sales are thinking from day to day. My experience leads me to believe that to get superior results from your sales team you must set up a compensation program to pay an accelerated commission rate once any salesperson has met their annual goals. Challenge them to do more, and be willing to reward them handsomely. Also, do not ever go back on a promise to pay as it will live with you forever, and any program after that will be suspect.

When you have high achievers on your sales team, you must keep them and continue to motivate them regularly. You must also never pull something away that has been promised or laid out as a reward if something is achieved. This is not always money as it could be a new office, computer, car, or just a plain and simple reward of any type when someone has overachieved in obtaining more sales revenues for the company.

I want to focus on sales compensation and later will tell you of an incident that happened to me, the "sales"-compensation-minded person.

I went through many plans over my years. Normally, salespeople are paid salaries and commissions with sometimes year-end bonuses. Now, there are many combinations of this and you can set up a program that works for your company or industry. What I am trying to do is just emphasize how important this whole compensation issue is should you want to beat your revenue plan year after year along with creating an industry-leading sales team. Why do I emphasize achievers? The main reason is that you must have as many overachievers as possible on your sales team to win in today's environment. A compensation program for revenue growth is one immediate way to tell what type of people you have on your team. This does not mean each and every year all of your sales team will hit the home run. What will happen is that a strong team will be motivated and focused throughout the year to win more rewards, whatever they may be. When you introduce a plan to pay extra for additional sales you will get a very positive response from the high achievers. Those salespeople who are a bit taken back would be the ones you need to watch closely as you implement this plan. You do not need people who question an aggressive plan like this on your sales team. Move them to another group or out of the company. Now, if all you want is a good salesperson who fills out reports, works fairly hard, and tells you what you want to hear, then by all means pay them a salary and small bonus. I expected and demanded we exceed our sales plans every year, which is what makes the whole sales effort fun and rewarding!

So at a sales meeting, we presented our new compensation plan which consisted of the following:

- Salary, which was 60-70 percent of total basic pay
- Commission, which was the other 30-40 percent of the total package
- Extended commission, which was more compensation based on additional revenues

This is fairly simple even though the difficulty is in the details. It must be explained thoroughly to each salesperson so they will understand how the company is taking care of them and what is expected from them. The base pay is easy as this is simply the annual amount broken down into pay periods and a type of guarantee. This is needed for financial security even though the rest of the package must be explained and understood so that security becomes less of an issue. The commission is based on expected sales in a given area of responsibility. Your compensation team will know the expected forecast for a given geography as you put the annual budgets together. This plan also forces your sales management to review and understand your company's salespersons territory potential and forecasts for growth. Once these are broken down, it is simple to take the revenue numbers and put a simple percentage or territory factor on them to come up with the commission rates for your teams. Each salesperson normally knows their territory and how much revenue performance they will need to meet their piece of the company budget. When they meet 100 percent of the territory revenue goal assigned to them, then they will get fully compensated on salary and standard commission listed previously. Part of the challenge is organizing this plan and remembering that all people tend to have different plans according to employment longevity, territory, along with previous income history. You now have what I call the base compensation which I define as the amount of money the salesperson can be very comfortable with achieving if they do an acceptable job in their assigned job. This also motivates them to meet their territory plan, which contributes to the overall goals of the company. This will also satisfy the company management and finance team as sales group can now define in detail the amount of compensation to budget for when the sales team achieves the company sales revenue plan.

Finance departments are always interested to join in sales compensation planning, and I suggest doing just that and have them join the compensation planning team. You want them involved so there are no surprises and the plan is fair and solid. You need their buy-in to make sure you have budget dollars and no one, through the year, is able to take back money promised to the sales team or try to change the plan as the year progresses.

Now, it is time to explain the details of the third item which is the extended commission or, if you wish to call it, a bonus. It is fully based on exceeding company revenue plans. Each salesperson could be encouraged and motivated to sell as much as possible in their respective territories. An additional compensation plan should be in place to reward a salesperson when they exceed their assigned goals. I suggest an accelerated or multiple plan which is defined as paying a larger commission rate for sales over assigned individual plans. Once a salesperson meets their plan, a larger percentage commission is paid on all sales above this number. This is a great opportunity for high achievers to realize a reward while equally the company sees expanded revenue growth over the annual plan.

So here I was my first year on the job as VP sales presenting to the company management team the new compensation plan I was preparing for my first sales meeting with the entire sales team. Once I showed everyone how the base salary and commission part works and they agreed it met finance budget for sales team payroll, I went into the accelerated commission presentation. I knew this would be a challenge and was prepared for resistance. Here are just a few of the questions:

1. What happens if half of the sales team misses plan and a few of the others make plan while the rest exceed plan but we still do not make

the overall plan? We would not only miss the overall plan but also pay out more to the higher achievers, right?

2. You mean a salesperson has no cap on how much they can make?

3. How does the company justify a program that opens up so much opportunity to the sales team and not to others?

Let me tell you how I responded to each of these:

1. If half the team misses plan, we have a problem anyway, right? This plan gives us the chance to make up lost revenues in other areas by motivating the other salespeople. This plan will help us make plan without going out with programs to get more orders. These emergency programs normally focus on reducing our prices on certain product lines or some other means to achieve additional orders. These usually end up costing us margin and more dollars than we would ever pay on the accelerated plan to the salespeople who would achieve more orders. One additional comment was that this program creates an environment of pier pressure on the entire sales team. This alone creates an environment that is healthy for all involved as it brings out the best in the winners and exposes the weak.

What we witnessed over the years of doing this plan is that some salespeople did fall short. With this said, between the salespeople who met their goals and the ones that exceeded them, we exceeded the company plan. We also had years where we exceeded the plan by numbers we could not have imagined at the start of the year. I suggested time and again it is better to challenge the sales team with this positive program rather than have knee-jerk year-end programs that deteriorate company margins and set the stage for lower pricing and more of these programs in the years to come.

2. Yes, no cap on the amount they can make. By the way, the company also has no cap! Once the company makes plan, increased profit expands at a greater rate on these additional revenue dollars. I was no finance person, but it was easy math when much of the expense

is included in the annual plan and additional revenues over this plan bring accelerated profits. Everyone wins.

I was part of commission programs that actually caused de-motivational problems for high achievers. I remember a few times a salesperson exceeded plan by 50-80 percent because of a big order that came in. The salesperson had worked hard on this opportunity and was told the order was too big to pay even normal commission. The conclusion was to offer the salesperson a commission at a reduced rate, not even the normal rate! Can you imagine the feeling the salesperson and sales team had when this was announced? The company made out big, the salesperson took a negative hit on a positive success. The real issue is when you work the math; orders brought in that exceed the revenue plan do allow the company to pay more in commission to the salespeople responsible for these increased revenues.

3. The sales team is different from other company personnel who work in different company departments. This program does not prevent any department from having motivational programs for their teams. Sales are responsible for revenue, and their mentality is money reward. The company and its employees should be proud of a program and a sales team that continues to grow revenue and keep all of them employed.

The support engineering team reported to me when I was VP sales and support in Japan. I remember one time when we were scheduling reviews and raises. As a good sales leader, I received approval for some nice salary raises for the engineers. I was ready for the first review, and when we finished, I informed the particular engineer the great news about salary raise. The look on his face was one of "so what, but thanks." I was confused and a bit angry as "I" had gotten this raise for them and they should be shaking my hand. Well, a few days passed and I received a call from the U.S. headquarters. They were concerned that one of the engineers had not cashed his checks and this had been for six months. I got the name, and guess what? Yes, it was the ungrateful one I had just given a raise to! I cautiously approached this person and asked about the checks. This person apologized and explained to me that his checks were under the mattress at home and they would be cashed the next day. This was a huge lesson for guess who? Money was not the real motivator in this person's case as we were paying him well and within his needs. Two weeks later, I called this person in to see how things were going. I also had just received additional permission for new computers and informed him of this. This person jumped out of the chair, gave me a huge handshake, and left with a smile that almost could not fit through the door. I again became very aware of what motivates people in different positions within the company and became much better at this evaluation of needs.

This sales compensation plan I have presented is just one of many. It worked well, and many internal departments gave their input as the years went by. I encourage any company to come up with a similar plan; just make sure you continue to keep in mind that the plan must be focused and motivated to exceed the company plan. If it is focused on making the standard results, then that is what you will get. I found it to be very important to make adjustments to your compensation plan annually. This forces your team to review the plan with company management and also establish the budget with finance. You also need to keep the plan fresh and motivational for the sales team. As I suggested earlier, it is really a good idea to have your finance team understand the plan as you and the sales team need their assistance throughout the year. To get new ideas for enhancing the compensation plan, why not ask a few select salespeople how they like the program and encourage suggestions on what could make it even better. This is where we came up with the best positive changes, and when putting them together and presenting them at the annual meeting, it was always nice to explain where the ideas came from for the changes.

Most companies have policies to hold formal reviews with all employees each year. Reviewing sales teams is made easier if the focus is on revenues and items associated with growing the company sales. There was a year we were told that we had to focus on more than just sales-related items for reviews of the sales team. Of course, we wondered why this was the case as there were already enough items on the review sheets and we did not need to add some that were not relevant to getting orders. The ones we focused on, which were normally good review subject material, were

- Sales growth of a given territory.
- Supporting all company product lines.
- Relationship building with inner company departments especially marketing.
- Time management in and out of office.
- Working with channels and customers.
- Personal growth and training.

Now we were instructed to discuss others with high priority such as filling out expense reports, watching the budget for their territory even more closely, being too critical of company departments such as customer service and shipping, and others like these. The big question was why as none of this encouraged revenue growth and all of them could be handled if there was a specific problem. Why address them at an annual review if not needed? You need to make sure that reviews for the sales team are associated with what is really important to grade the salesperson and these are directly related to revenue growth for the company. This is the time to motivate the achievers and give notice of concern to the underachievers. If you allow yourself to muddy the water with other mundane items, you will end up with the wrong message for the entire team.

The reason I am putting reviews in this area with compensation is because it is a perfect time to discuss the compensation program and get any questions, comments, or suggestions on the table. As discussed earlier, great salespeople relate to the compensation plan and love to talk about it. We came up with new ideas from them and implemented many of their observations to improve the plan each year. It ended up many times being motivational as the team got excited when they saw their ideas being incorporated into their plan.

Salespeople are in the field week after week by themselves. What better way to make them become more loyal and bond to each other than to let them see how they contributed to a company plan.

As we were preparing for the annual sales meeting, we kept running into a wall as to how we could create more interest in new product promotions as the sales team already had a full plate. Some of the meeting centered on punishment for those that did not meet assigned goals. This could go as far as probation or eventual termination of some salespeople. We then set back and really looked at what we were doing and decided to contact a few salespeople to get their input as to why it is so hard to get attention for new promotions. We did not attack them but just called and asked what, if they were us, they would do to get the new products going forward. I was not surprised by the feedback, and by the end of five to six of these calls, the whiteboard had items on it we had not even considered and not one of them was probation or termination. We also suspected the people we called would be in contact with others in the field telling them what had happened on the call. The word spread, and the sales team knew they were on a highly visible hot seat in the coming year to get these programs moving forward. There was also curiosity in the field as to how we were going to encourage them. It ended up being a program that came from the field, and it was based quarterly and goals were given out in retrospect to territory and customer opportunity based on sales management recommendations. The compensation part was entirely new and not based on money but on rewards that were thought up through the phone conversations. We had immediate acceptance from the team as they knew it was a hot topic and now were being rewarded to make these new product programs successful.

Be creative with your sales compensation program as this is a great way to motivate a team to exceed the many challenges handed down to them. This is not only the annual goal but situations that come up throughout the year. I remember many times we had to go to the sales team and ask them for additional attention for certain product sales shortfalls. They would always respond positively because they were treated the right way and were fundamentally pleased with the compensation and treatment the company was giving them. You give me a sales team that is not making plan and complains about any additional requests, and I will tell you to go right to the compensation program targeted for the sales group and you will see why they act like this. This is the same for your top sales achiever. You should never intentionally irritate or de-motivate your top achievers. This does not mean you cannot challenge or correct them, but do not tinker with the things that make them top achievers. These people are very loyal to you as long as you take good care of them. The company must realize who these people are and make sure they pay attention to them. Sometimes these people are called "franchise people" and for good reason. When motivated and compensated correctly, they will time after time perform at the top of the team. They are also known in the industry as top performers and are always being courted by others. This also is not to say these people do not occasionally leave so while you have them, run them hard and enjoy the results.

If you are really serious, and I emphasize serious, about exceeding your sales plans, then you must motivate your sales team and constantly evaluate them to make sure you have the best in the industry. Your company cannot put compensation roadblocks up and then also expect positive results from the sales team.

We went to the sales meeting expecting a great time with our team as we had just had a very good year and exceeded the sales plan. Everyone from the sales group was expecting a positive meeting with the product groups and also good news on our compensation for the upcoming year. The meeting took place for the entire week, and during this time, we were wondering when we would see our new individual compensation packages. The week went by and no mention of the "package." Each night after dinner and during social time, this quickly began to be the number one topic; and by midweek, we were starting to really wonder why we had not seen our new program. Of course, the conversation was turning ugly so the foundation was already set that the new package must be questionable at best. Well, Friday came along and finally we were told we would get our envelopes with the new compensation package enclosed on the way out of the meeting as we were on our way to the airport. Why would anyone ever do this? We got the envelopes and climbed aboard the bus. By the time we got to the airport, people were going crazy. The new compensation package was not even close to what everyone was expecting, especially after having a great year. The program was negative and a setback from the current plan, and no one spent the time to tell us why or at least explain to us the plan to see if we were missing something. We all got on the plane and arrived home with negative attitudes and many questions with the weekend ahead of us to stew. By Monday, the phones at corporate were ringing off the hook with concerns and questions. The management took the plan and changed it that week, and in total, it turned out positive a few weeks later.

Her are some points:

1. The sales meeting over the week turned from positive to negative.
2. The people were thinking about the new compensation plan (remember what is the most important thing to a salesperson), which kept their minds away from some good business presentations.
3. People became more negative over the weekend, and everything turned bad the next week with most of that week lost due to everyone concerned and complaining about their new compensation plan.
4. The plan was changed which caused more defocus for another time frame as the new plan was being introduced and explained over the phones.

Why wait to present the most important subject to a salesperson when you get the team together? If you have a bad plan, then shame on you as you have plenty of time before a meeting to leak out to a few what might be coming and then get feedback. Why take a chance of turning a meeting which costs so much time and money into a negative event? I suggest getting the plan out first thing in the morning of the first day. Announce the general plan to all participants then break out with the people in groups or alone. Get the feedback then have management reconvene that evening and settle any issues. Issues could be individual where you missed something for a person, or it could be team wide where you just forgot to consider something. The next morning, get the program cleaned up, meet with any individuals, and get going in a positive direction for the rest of the week. I guarantee by the end of the week, you will send them home motivated and ready to slay orders.

One last thing on salespeople and how to get them to constantly think about spending more time selling for the company. As a manager, you must think of many ways to motivate and encourage your team to exceed their expectations. I had a lot of fun with my sales team in taking out their spouses for a nice dinner whenever we could find time. It was even better if we had a couples' function, and I had a chance to approach more of them as a group. I would ask them how things were going, how are the kids, etc. Then I would ask the simple question, "How do you like the compensation program we have for your spouse?" You could see the eyes bug out a bit and then the feedback would begin and the fun would start. I would find out how many really understood the program and then give a high-level explanation to it while adding a few details as to the acceleration part of the package. I would then ask them how they liked the fact that the program would allow any salesperson to make a lot more money if they just beat their goals. This helped keep the focus on the accelerated commission program. Well, by the time my salespeople were into the conversation, it was too late and I was already encouraging the spouses to start planning for new things around the house. The following are things I would mention now to the spouses:

- What type of new car are you planning on buying this year?
- How is the furniture in your house? You really should get some new things if you have a chance.
- What about thinking of a new house in the next year or so as if you are planning a family? It is best to get set up now.
- Now, just where are you going for that holiday vacation?

Of course this was all fun, but very effective as I know in many cases the pressure that the spouse put on to get more orders was by far much more than anything the company could do. I also can tell you who some of the most aggressive spouses were as the next time I saw them they would tell me about some things they had gotten since the last time we talked. Sales can be a lot of fun!

Always do your best to constructively interact and support company teams as the alternative is the biggest time waster in corporations today

Chapter 3

Successful Company Teams Work Together

So how does a company encourage its different departments to work on successful communications to grow business? Understand I asked successful, not positive, nice, or condescending communications. Success within the company relies on constructive conversations among teams. This starts at the top, and the team will follow the leaders of their group.

When I was young in my sales career, I learned quickly that the sales team was under a watchful eye from many departments within the company. I went to numerous meetings, and at some point, when things got testy and there was a problem, blame had to be assigned to someone. The people at the meeting entered scramble mode and hoped their name or department was not getting the "blame monkey" put on their back. I would start to write down things I could counterattack with in case someone would start questioning me or someone on the sales team. I do admit I was just as bad and am sorry for the attacks I launched on some individuals. This is very damaging to the company and must be derailed by top management the minute it becomes visible.

Over time some people get better at handling these types of situations whereas some never do and others never want to as this is their way of gaining power. Of course, if top management is in attendance, then some people take this as an opportunity to crucify their person of choice. I saw through a lot of this as I became more seasoned, and I even witnessed top management subtly encouraging this behavior with their teams. If someone had to be accused, then it would not be them or their team. As I grew in my profession, I began to realize how this whole process was a waste of time and I started to implement an environment with my sales team to change this interaction. I emphasize it took me many years and it was not until way late in my career I finally achieved this attitude. I am hoping just by stating this fact you will move into this behavior more quickly as it will enhance your daily attitude and create a more positive work environment.

We are all responsible for company success so why not just solve the problem together. The challenge is to instill this attitude in all people in the company. So in my later years as the leader of my teams, I encouraged my teams to be open, honest, and respectful to other company employees. I am sure at times I came across to others not this way so it is important to try your best to practice this behavior at all times. Of course, when I was with my sales people in a meeting, I could help this behavior, but being there is not always possible. If I found out about an incident, I would discuss the situation with my team member and try to give them ideas on how to handle the situation in the future. If one person was a constant violator of this type of interaction, then I would get more forceful with them and keep a closer eye on them while continuing to encourage improvement.

In one instance we had a large promotion coming up so I had some of my sales team into the office to talk about how we were going to be successful promoting it to our customers. Within a few minutes, the complaints from my team started in:

- They never asked us for our input as to this promotion.
- There are no training or communications packages to help us prepare.
- How can we do this when they have us focusing on all the other things we must do to grow the other product lines?
- This is just another time-wasting effort that will take us away from our normal duties and also upset our channels and customers with promotion meetings which will have no positive outcome.

You will usually hear the same type of objections, just sometimes in a different format. Over the years, I came up with a good answer to all these concerns. Get on the phone, or get a team meeting with all parties involved to air things out. Do not get personal, and do not attack the programs; just get the issues on the table. The management then must cooperate in the meeting and be referees in helping the teams come up with solutions to the concerns.

This type of situation occurs often with the sales team, especially when an internal company team comes up with a program with no input from the people who have to implement the tasks. Many times leads to a launch that does not meet the expectations of the company management. This does not have to happen if people would just include the people responsible for implementation up-front to prepare and understand the program. When a product promotion does not go well many times it gets high visibility and company management is now directly involved as to why things are not on track. One of the biggest mistakes company management makes at this juncture, and it happens all the time, is when a product promotion is not going well and they do not want to listen to the real issues. Management is presented the issues but do not really hear them and then someone must take the blame for not meeting the company's goals. In my example earlier, I talked about how to encourage teams to be more positive and work closer with other department teams. This will only go so far without the same attitude from the management team. So top management must also strive to set a good example and work together. This was more difficult for me than trying to change my own team's habits. I found that with some peers you have great success while with others it is always a work in progress. Politics can be an issue; hidden agendas along with less-than-honest interactions can be a setback within this process. You must try to identify in your mind who you feel can positively work with you and your team on issues to resolution. This is not hard to do if you really observe through your ear and eye senses how people act with you one-on-one and then in a group environment. Group environments can be with their own team, other teams, and with top company management. The company management team is the real test as this is when you can really witness what people are made of and also what their real agenda is.

Once you define this area, you can begin your work. The people that want to really make the company successful will be very open to working with others to get things moving in the right direction. The people that want to make themselves successful are the ones that I had the most difficult time with. They will change their minds in a minute if their boss or some other top manager has different ideas or disagrees with a path to move forward. We use to call these people "yes-men or women," and they were known as this throughout the company.

Most people will work positive with you once they know you are honest and non-aggressive toward them. This includes people that do not really understand the sales process but have the company success and goals as something they want to be a part of. Getting these people to help in the sales process makes them feel even more part of the overall success. Thankfully, most companies have a high percentage of these people so I found sitting with them, including them in our discussions, and asking their opinions very key to getting them to support the sales team.

The more difficult is that last group, the "yes-men or women." I found that it is very hard to be totally successful with this group and it is a process that must always be in motion. I would meet with these people one-on-one on a regular basis. This is the hard part as you never know what their real agenda is so you try to establish some kind of base understanding with them. Once they understand why you are there and what the "subject" of the day is, you can state your case while being very clear on what you are trying to accomplish. When it comes to a larger meeting, it is a bit more difficult to move forward with these types of personalities. Most of the time when they are presented with a decision to make, they want to check with someone else or think about it. These people are notorious for delaying, changing, or just not making decisions. This is where the one-on-one comes into real play. Once they know your position, then it is time to casually present this position to their boss and/or other top management. I suggest going to the more influential managers as there still are "yes-men or women" in this upper management group. In sales, you do not have time for too many games if you are driven to be successful. It is your job to obtain support for your programs from key management personnel who will support the programs you and your team want to pursue. At some point, these managers will be approached for their opinions on sales team direction. Being that you set the right trap lines, the situation you want will then be supported by these executives and it is time to bring closure by getting everyone together for agreement to move forward. This takes time and effort, but any effective salesperson will always be looking for buy-in for their ideas to increase sales revenues. If you have sales people that are not doing just this with you or someone in the company, then you should be concerned as to their drive to excel in their job. You will also find it takes ongoing improvement of listening and observation skills to get to this point. As you practice and improve your skills in this interpersonal strategy, it becomes much easier and thus you can get buy-in much quicker to help the company meet their objectives.

Remember, the items you are normally going after will need to be approved by some type of company team. At times, you have the ability to make your own decision, but it never hurts to have a few people you trust to take a look at your ideas. There is nothing better than honest feedback, and many times it enhanced something I was prepared to implement while also saving me from making some stupid mistakes. The real key is to have your team understand the importance of cooperation, and conversely, the negative results that happen when you have inner company fighting. Management must show the example, and the teams must be encouraged and taught how to work together. I am not naïve enough to know this ideal situation is very difficult to achieve. There are times that top management believes all is just great in the ranks below them. Many times this is not the case so it is the rank and file of the company that must try their best to cooperate and get things moving forward. It is the responsibility of every employee to show example, not talk and rumor negatively about each other. The key is to try to stay as positive as possible in a stressful environment and work positively with each other. The strongest example is when you as an individual learn how to work in difficult environments and come up with a solution to a company issue. So many times all I heard were the issues without solutions. I tremendously valued people who would not only state an issue but immediately follow up with a solution in order to solve this issue.

This leads to a discussion on meetings and relationships. As a manufacturer, this can be with customers and channels for your products to the market. These are two very important groups as without them your business would be nonexistent. If you are a channel to market for a manufacturer, then your two most important groups are the customer and manufacturer you represent. These groups are very important and should be treated like royalty whenever you meet with them, especially at your location. They are guests, and you have their 100 percent attention so take advantage of it. This also gives the sales team a great opportunity to get other departments involved and again improve relations. Defining the right people to meet with these visitors does take time as any given situation is usually different. You must also be very careful to your choices as you could be missing a great opportunity to bring someone in that adds to a certain interest which others do not view as important. Let's face it; some people are better at personal interaction than others. Then again just because someone is not a toastmaster speaker does not mean they cannot add value to a visit from the outside. The sales team must not only set the agenda but also lay out what needs to be said and not said. Many internal people take offense to this at times, and they must understand there are reasons to follow this guidance. Past history, current issues, and just plain customer personalities are very important considerations. This again is where people who have not been in sales take offense to a salesperson telling them what to do. The salesperson must take time before the meeting either face-to-face or on the phone to take control of these meetings. I have witnessed many of these meetings go down the wrong path because of one minor slip from a presenter or tour guide or hospitality host. When things go right, it almost always end up with more business over time, so take these opportunities seriously. These opportunities do not occur often as the customer, channel teams, and manufacturers are very busy, so get the right people involved and prepare extensively. This also an opportunity to bring the entire team together as after a positive successful meeting there is always tighter bonding with all who participated. We all like to feel good and win, and when we do this, relationships turn more positive.

To conclude, company management has the responsibility to be very aware of how the different teams are working together. They must not take sides even though there is a tendency to protect their given team and at times they should. Positive management meetings are a good way to start a process that will flow down to others. When hearing someone talk down about another team or person on a business issue, confront the situation. Find out why the feeling is there and move to solve it. Take the poison out of the company may it be the person who is always complaining or just a plain negative attitude. For a company to win and meet goals there must be an awareness and acceptance that inter-company cooperation makes everyone a winner.

A sales team must promote customers internally as they are ultimately the most important factor for long term business growth.

Chapter 4

Growing the Customer Base

Sales group is responsible to keep existing customers while adding new ones. This is plain and simple and always very difficult. You must promote new products even when at times they do not fit the total needs of your customer. Sales must listen to complaints from the customer about the service they are not getting and then smooth things over even though most of the time the salesperson would like to air the same complaints. The customer normally goes directly to their salesperson for every question as that is the person they trust the most. These are all opportunities to lock up all possible business with customers buying from you currently. The other challenge is finding time to pursue new customers. These are the primary ways to not only meet but exceed your sales revenue goals as a salesperson. Sounds simple, so if it is, then everyone should be in sales and simply strive to meet these two strategies, right?

I was in my first month of a new sales position, and my territory responsibilities were then assigned. One customer, I was told, had been called on by many past salespeople from our company and there were never any sales orders received so it was always passed along to the new salesperson. I was the new guy and the boss told me it was a large account but just a bit difficult to break into, so I went out the door for the first visit to them. I was determined to stay with this account until I had success. I needed to do something different and was fired up and ready to penetrate this account. Upon entering, the lobby was constructed of large polished wooden walls and very crowded with what I viewed as other salespeople. I waded through the crowd toward the reception desk and informed the receptionist of my scheduled appointment. I was told to take a seat and they would contact me when ready. Another salesperson came through the door and asked for the same person; they were escorted directly through the large door that I hoped someday I would get through to see what was on the other side. I waited for what seemed to be hours then the person I was scheduled to see was in front of me. I was politely told it was nice I came by and to leave my "stuff" on the desk area and he would pick it up when returning from lunch. Then he went with the other salesperson that had come in after me.

Every salesperson has experiences like this. This is the tough and lonely part of sales, and the ones that can make it through this are the people you want on your team. Customers are tough, and salespeople must find ways to strengthen relations with existing ones and break into new ones. Let's discuss existing customers and ways to strengthen relations.

I found lack of listening as the number one complaint customers had of the salespeople who visited them. They wanted to be polite and let the salespeople show their stuff, but they also had their issues and wanted to get those presented and solved. I witnessed many times a customer trying to get a point across only to be overrun by a sales pitch. I also saw many an opportunity laid on the table by a customer only to be left there by an non-observant salesperson. This is the easiest way to lose a customer, by not letting them set the agenda for your interactions. The key to keeping a customer is fairly easy, but it is very seldom discussed unless you have some senior salespeople who are given the opportunity to teach the rookies. Just listen and take care of what the customers view as important to them at the moment in time. Salespeople have plenty of time to promote and sell new ideas and products, and it becomes much easier once you take the customer issues off the table. Again, this is very difficult and this is why so many salespeople fail at keeping and growing existing customers not to mention trying to add new ones.

How do you know if you are doing a good job for your customer? Many times a salesperson does not sell their total product offerings to their existing customers. What does a salesperson do if the customer is not buying all the products possible from your company? A good idea is to define where you are with a particular customer. Earlier in this book I explained how a report could focus on this type of information to get a clear picture of how the company is doing with total customer coverage. Usually a company has core products that are larger in market share than others. The stronger products also normally dictate who your main customers are. By this, I mean the customers that are giving you the most business are normally the ones buying your high market share or larger revenue-generating products.

Keeping existing customers who buy these products is of utmost importance, and at times a sales team is hesitant to promote risky new products to these customers as they do not meet the perceived customer expectations. A salesperson is a bit hesitant to sell a product that might disappoint a customer and thus risk losing the existing business. When looking at a simple customer spreadsheet, which was presented in previous chapters, and defining what products they are currently buying from your company, the opportunities for other products you produce stick out clearly. The big challenge is to find out why they are not buying all your products and deal with each one so you can either set a strategy to sell it or decide the product is not right at this time. This sounds so easy to do, so why is it that many companies do not put heavy focus on this type of analysis? The following are some reasons or, better yet, realities:

1. Rather than approach an existing customer with new products when they may be buying a comparable one from the competition, it is easier and less stressful to spend time promoting the company's core/high market share products to new customers.

2. The products that are not leaders in revenue are usually not viewed as leading products in the market. When taking a product to a customer who is using a market-leading product, it is very difficult to break this habit and have them change. The customer has made a choice, so the challenge is to convince them it is time to change or upgrade—a very sensitive situation.

3. Companies get caught up in putting heavy emphasis on promoting the product of choice by the top management. This means products will change position of importance year over year according to what

management deems as being the new product we must sell more of. The sales team must always promote the new offerings, but many times the company must give the sales team a product that has advantages over a product that is currently a competitive market leader. It is seldom that a company comes up with a new never-offered-before product, so the challenge to sales is find ways to wedge their way into a customer and relationships are key in this battle.

These are just a few examples, and this does mean that a company should not have a focused strategy when it comes to promoting products to existing customers. Why promote a product to a good customer when they may not see it beneficial to their environment? Even though the answer to this is that we should never promote a product to existing customers that does not fit their needs, companies continue to do it time over time. This irritates a good customer, wastes valuable sales time, and causes internal conflict between sales and other company groups. If we now go back and review why we do not sell all product lines to all of a company's existing customers, it becomes clearer. Many times customers have made choices to buy other company's products. Maybe it was that your company just missed the timing and was late to the market. It could be that the product you offer is not the best on the market and the customer wants to buy the best. There are many other reasons; and the real opportunity here is to list existing customers, what they buy and do not buy, and then realistically figure out what the next step is to maintain and grow business at all customers with their best interest in mind.

I have seen top management push salespeople to promote products to customers when the salesperson knew the timing was not right. I have seen customers pushed into buying a product that still was not ready for their application and resulted in a negative situation for all parties involved. The main point here is that company management team must do a review of their existing customers and promote what is right for them, not what is right for the company offering the product. There is nothing more irritating to a customer who is buying a good amount of your products than to be pushed into buying a product from you that is inferior to what is on the market or that they are currently using.

It was the start of the year, and we selected a few key salespeople with customers who were the largest users of our products. The meeting was to discuss how to sell some of the new offerings coming out from our company over the next few months. The company had invested a lot of money into these products, and even though we were late to the market, we had to give it our best to try to sell them. The sales team was reluctant to approach their good customers as they were already buying a good amount of our company's products and the new products were similar to the ones that were already in the market and being used successfully by their customers. Top management had dictated that all top customers should be on the list to visit, and the sales team was taking issue to this. Why irritate or even insult existing customers by pushing the new products on them? They were happy with what they were using as they were with products they bought from us, and their time was very valuable so don't waste it. The more we discussed a strategy, the more we were convinced there were better ways to attack this situation than to just blanket our existing customers of which many were happy with their current choices. This is not to say that we would not introduce and promote positively these new products; we just knew the outcome would not meet the demands of our company management for projected sales revenues. We laid out a plan for both existing and potentially new customers, many of who were not using any of our product lines. We knew we would have to balance our time selling these products and try to establish the most effective way to meet our sales plan assignments. We also needed to be very keen on when to exit and move on to another customer. We had to put together the process of what happens next and make sure, especially with existing customers, we knew when to back off as we did not want to negatively affect our other business with them. One other important thing this program pointed out over time was the fact that some products were not the right fit in the current environment for some customers. Without a very focused but simple sales reporting process, which even at times does not convince the company management, the sales team will be accused of not putting the effort into the new promotions.

Using this sales strategy is very productive when it is kept on the front burner and followed very closely by the teams involved. It allows the sales team to choose and focus on accounts they believe will win them orders. The management teams working the promotion must respond and assist the sales team on the action items that are listed, and the priority must focus in this area. When the timing is right and the plan is set, you have a great chance of winning the business be it with existing or new potential customers. Because of this, everyone must be very sensitive to the environment and ready to move quickly when the opportunity arises. A simple reporting format is needed in many more places within companies as there is so much happening that no one has a chance to react to the most critical ones as quickly as they should.

The sales team also should be involved in the timing and release of any major promotional program to the customers. They know the customers, and it is critical to present any new products to them at the right time in their business cycle. You must not blame customers if they do not take the bait and buy. Realize the customer is very busy, and if they have no need, it is much more difficult to convince them to give you the time to listen to your proposal. You have an opportunity to use customer feedback, should you choose, to honestly look at what you are offering and adjust to the market for the next move.

Another area that has always been a challenge involves your competition as it relates to customers. Many people have written books and preached about how important it is that salespeople know the competition and their products sometimes in great depth. Many feel the salesperson should be very well educated on their competitors, and much money is spent by companies in doing this. Well, I have a very different view, so let me explain and please hear me out. I do agree that a company should rely on too much competitive information especially when planning to form a product or channel strategy. They must keep up on what the competition is offering and how they are offering it such as certain promotions or products releases. This is about as far as I am willing to go with trying to know the competition especially from the sales team's perspective. I can prove over and over that you do not need to educate your sales team on competitive products for them to be successful. I challenge anyone on this, and I find the best way to find out about your competition is not to find out. This sounds confusing, and why would I be putting this type of discussion in the customer chapter of this book? That is exactly where you will find out about your competition—at the customers.

When you get right down to it, what does the salesperson have for their main job function? Selling the company's offerings! Who do they sell to? The customer base! Then all they need to do is find out what the customer wants and give it to them and they will buy. Think of it in your everyday life when you want to buy something. It is the product or salesperson who takes your need and finds a solution that makes it easy for you to commit. The sales team meets their assigned duties and the company flourishes. Okay, I know there is now disagreement on this as I am challenging a very sensitive area of business practices. Let me back this up with more supporting evidence. With the complexity of today's products and services along with companies demanding more out of their employees, many salespeople have a difficult time knowing their own core products in depth. This does not even include all the other things they need to know about their company as they are swamped with information weekly. They are constantly challenged with new products of their own along with enhancement of current product offerings. So how do they find time or why do they need to know about the competitive product in any kind of depth? They are selling their products to their customers. The products have been designed by their companies' teams who did the research to assure they were giving the sales team a product that is in the most part equal to or better than any of the competitors. Now, take a look at the poor customer. Not only do they have the challenge of knowing their own job duties they now have to know the companies they buy from in many different areas and also the products of each of these companies and how they fit their needs. No way is it possible; so many customers rely on receiving this information from the salespeople who visit or call on them.

A great signal to look for from a salesperson who is floundering is when they get into the whirlpool of "meeting the competitors' offerings." This is the sign of a salesperson who has just visited a customer who also was just visited by another salesperson from a competing company. This competing salesperson filled the customer with many facts about how their product was better than any other. They filled the customer with all this information on what their product does (even if he does not need the feature), and the customer is now an expert on the competitors' products. Now, your salesperson walks in and gets hit with all this information and goes into the customer whirlpool, which goes around and around as you fight to meet the perceived competitor's offering. The customer continues to throw out the competitor's features as he has been instructed to do by your competitor while you continue to try and keep from going deeper into the whirlpool. This is the deadliest trap a salesperson can allow themselves to be brought into. There is only one way out, and it works every time. The simple question to the customer is, "what is it that you need from this product to meet application?" This helps the salesperson move to the next step and get out of this "chase the competition" situation. If the customer does not want to cooperate and get on with what they need, then this is also a positive situation. This tells an attentive salesperson it is time to move on to another discussion totally and maybe even call it a day and get on to the next customer quickly. Most products I have sold have numerous features that customers will never use or do not need. With that in mind, some customers need feature 1 and 2 but not 3 and 4 whereas another customer needs feature 1, 2, and 3. This is not all bad, and this is why your development people spend time listing product features and benefits. What is important is that most of your competitors also have these features and at times they have similar or different ones. This is why you must ask the customer what they need so you can focus on this and not a competing product. Rather than go back to your design team asking to meet the competitor's offering (the black hole), ask them to assist you in focusing on the customer who has committed to buy it once we meet their needs. I have seen many a salesperson and company change, add, and enhance products for customers throwing up roadblocks via the competitive product only to never get the order after upgrades has been added. This is ultimately the salesperson's responsibility, and a salesperson must focus on the specific customer requirements and also get a commitment that if these are done, there will be a high probability for an order. It is very refreshing and much less frustrating to the entire team to approach this competitive strategy in this way.

This is also a great way to define who your customer "go to" person is. Many a customer has what I call "road blockers" who give you every reason you could ever think of not to buy your products but just do not come out and tell you. Many times it can be defined quickly as these people constantly go back to comparing you with the competitor and when asked what they need, run around all over the place with no real answer. This is key to helping a salesperson recognize then locate and focus on the real decision maker and over time becomes a much more efficient and professional way to really run your customer strategies. A salesperson who does this is highly respected within their company as they do not waste valuable time with other teams chasing after an order that most of the time never materializes.

I entered an electronics store hoping to spend less than $1,000 on a new high-powered tuner. I needed to have a certain amount of wattage and the capabilities of powering six speakers for surround/theater sounds. I also had remote speakers on the other side of the house so I need to be able to program them to be on and off as needed. I was now in front of at least thirty different tuners with pricing and capabilities over a wide range. I was totally confused even though I had been doing research on what would fit my needs. Well, here comes the salesperson and I was hoping he would focus on my needs. After introductions, he asked the perfect question, "What is it you are trying to accomplish?" I was elated, and with a big smile I explained my needs. He quickly reduced the thirty or so tuners down to three or four. Now, we were getting somewhere, and the next step he took was to give me just a few highlights as to the comparison of the finalists. They all had what I needed; it was just some features that each had that were somewhat different. We talked a bit more and chose some "nice things to have for the future" and reduced it down to two. The choice then was cosmetic and price that ended up at $800, and the decision was made. Now, I have a great tuner and the only real problem is the instruction book is one hundred pages and I only use about 50 percent of what the unit can offer to me.

This was great work by this salesperson as a few other stores I visited the salespeople went right into a full-fledged competitive dump and I was confused in the first five minutes. The difference is that someone took the time to ask me what I needed and then made the fit work. This example probably happens to many people every day, so I reiterate the need to find out what the customer wants and minimize the competitive conversation; you will meet more success and have more time to sell.

If you are still a bit apprehensive about this, then please sit down, think it over, and why not give it a try. I will tell you one more time that no matter what you believe, your sales team does not have time to understand fully what they have for their own offerings, so why take up their time trying to make them competitive product experts? Define what it is the company really needs to know about the competitors at a high level and then go do it. I am always interested to see if a company sits down on a regular basis and reviews a list on what their key customers really need. If you do not, then try it for a change as it might surprise you. When you begin this practice of giving the customer exactly what they need, your time will be better spent doing exactly that and seeing your sales revenue grow.

When a sales team really understands their customer base, they know who and when to approach customers with new or enhanced product offerings. I have given you ideas on how to strengthen your relations with your existing customers by listening to what their situation is at given times. They will buy more and will use more of your new products when they see you more sensitive to their situation. By doing this, you will also have a very high percentage of retention of the business they are giving you. You will also build a relationship that will be hard for any competitor to break. The sales team must be confident to control the customer environment, and they must be forthcoming to tell the company what the customer can and will tolerate. This at times is difficult when the company wants the sales team to promote something that is just not right at the time for a selected customer. Inter-company trust is the most important thing to have at these times, and without it, I have seen many an ugly meeting take place. If a customer is pushed too hard toward something they do not want, it can be the beginning of a loyal customer moving to another solution which fits their needs closer than your offer.

How do you convert new customers over to your company as you continue to manage your existing ones? This is a challenge that every sales team has to face. Some of the ways to grow business year over year is to have innovative new products, customer expansions, robust economy, and converting customers to your products. I would like to focus on the last item as this is the key to growing business over the long run and also the most challenging. A salesperson becomes fairly comfortable with their current customers, and the closer they get, the easier it is to spend more time with them. The problem comes when the time spent is non-productive in the business or personal aspect. There comes a time when a salesperson becomes too comfortable with their existing customer base and begins to use this as an excuse as to why they do not have time to pursue new customers. They must not be allowed to do this. A good way to enforce this message is to include customer expansion at the start of each year's annual plan for a given territory. This again can be simple and must be followed closely. The sales team cannot be allowed to be comfortable with their existing customer base even if they are meeting their sales goals. The management must demand new customers on a continuous basis, and the sales team must be pushed out of the comfort zone and required to find new opportunities in their assigned territories. Relationships are key to customer retention, and they can also be very dangerous to a salesperson's time if they allow it to interfere with growing other customers or obtaining new ones. I will comment later on the importance of the personal side of a relationship and managing this with a customer.

The business side of a relationship is when a salesperson assists a customer in solving a problem by helping to enhance a customer situation, making their company more productive. Customers and salespeople are very busy, and there is a balance of how much time they have to spend with each other. This is something a salesperson must be aware of at all times, and it comes in different ways such as face-to-face time, e-mail time, or phone time. I have talked to many customers and at times they all have both positive and negative comments on salespeople who call on them. The ultimate goal is to get closer to a customer so they will tell you what they like and do not like about salespeople. The key is to find out what they like about salespeople who call on them and also why they try their best to avoid a difficult salesperson. By really listening, you should make sure not to be the next salesperson on his "avoid" list.

I am presenting this to point out that a salesperson must manage their time with each customer and avoid getting into a rut and doing the same thing time and time again. Each customer has different personalities, and the salesperson must sharpen their skills regarding managing the customer relation. The goal should be to strategize time management with all customers and then understand just how to spend the right amount of time with customers to keep them satisfied and buying your products. I want to state again that this is one of the most difficult tasks a salesperson has. It is fairly easy to visit and promote your products to a customer you have a good relationship with. The salesperson must take good care of all existing customers while carving out time to pursue new ones. It is difficult and often time consuming when going for a new discovery customer. I always found that the best way to enhance your sales skills was to break into a new customer account and try to obtain an order. This was the adrenaline pump from the sales perspective. It was always a big challenge, and the best salespeople will be the ones who take this challenge on and win new customers time and again. I am not talking about "cold calling" as we sometimes refer to it. I am talking about meeting a customer at some event or being introduced to them and then taking advantage of trying to find out if there is an opening to get a relationship established. In some businesses, I guess you must cold call, but I have found that the percentage of success compared to wasted time is unacceptable. Find different ways to meet new customers as this is very exciting to do. A salesperson must push themselves to create new customer opportunities as it is good for company growth but more importantly is good for the salesperson's mental well-being along with his back pocket.

I suggest the same format presented earlier to establish a plan of attack. One must look at customers as a whole and pick ones at a given time who may have a situation where your products will help them. This is not a sales call to introduce at random your product lines. It is a focused strategy to discover through your sources an opportunity to wedge yourself into an account in order to get an opportunity to perform. It is timing and understanding the situation, getting some inside information, and then getting to the right people who are in need of your assistance. This is another reason I am bullish on focused and simple reports. Sales teams must have time to dissect existing customers in order to understand the decision-making process. Likewise, they must have time to establish strategies for new customers if they are to expand the business for the company. By burdening the salespeople with unnecessary reports and non-sales-related tasks, the company is limiting their own growth potential.

We knew that one of our competitors was up for sale and the chance that another one of our competitors in the industry would have a good chance of merging with them. We first had our meeting to just talk about what might happen to the customer base if the merger would occur. We surmised that the merging companies would be a bit busy on the merger consolidation if it happened, and the sales team in particular might be concerned about the new organization. When a merger of a competitor is in the works, it is a great time to approach targeted customers buying the competitors products as they are curious and also possibly open to new ideas. I am not proposing ambulance chasing, so be careful how you approach any new customer in this situation. If they are current users of a product from one of the merging companies, they also most probably have relationships with them, and remember they chose to use that company's product for a reason. Back to my example, we thought it might be worth planning a strategy and the tactics associated based on this potential merger. We knew the merger might not occur, but if it did, there would be a small time frame in which we knew we could convert some major customers and distributors. We laid out the simple spreadsheet similar to the one in chapter one. We listed the accounts and distributors we thought were open for possible conversion. We then expanded this by laying out how we would approach each one quickly and make an offer they would find hard to refuse. We were gambling on the hunch that some of them would be confused and possibly upset with this merger while being open to trying something new.

We set timetables in detail such as what to do the "next" day after this merger was announced. We put into the equation what the dollar impact of new orders might be with each opportunity. We set teams up as to who would go, where, when, and what to discuss when they met these companies. We put together offers so as to take advantage of any openings if they occurred during the visit. We did not want to leave with the statement, "we will get back to you." This is a very important part of any customer conversion plan. Go with some ammunition; as my experience has been, the potential conversion customer will at some time in your initial meeting ask what the "deal" is. If you have nothing or are not ready to challenge them to "what they want," then it is a waste of both parties' time. Do not take this lightly as if you are to spend all this time getting ready for a conversion account sales call then go with the intent to drive home a win whenever there is an opening. The teams you send out must have fairly large approval power in this situation, so review different scenarios in your preparation meetings. Remember, this is when the adrenaline rushes and fun takes place.

Well, the merger took place, and I will never forget the next morning. The teams had airline tickets in hand, and everyone was excited. We hit the field over the next two weeks; it was long hours and extensive travel that we were prepared for. The whole company was involved, and the enthusiasm was tremendous. It was as we thought, the other companies were not even contacting the customers by phone as far as we could ascertain. It was an open door, and we took advantage of it. The conversion rate was more than we expected, and it led to a record-breaking year of orders and customer/distributor conversions.

Now these opportunities do not happen often, and when they do, you must be prepared to attack. This type of program can be used for any conversion program. We did this each year as you cannot wait just for a home run opportunity like this story. It will work in any situation, and it takes discipline and total company participation. You cannot have a customer conversion program from just the sales department. It must be embraced by top management, and if it is not, then the sales team should not go after it. You need to have your conversion arsenal fully stocked and be able to make decisions at any given moment as the door will close quickly. The effort level and time spent to bring in a new customer is very high. You steal valuable time from managing existing customers so you must make sure you have a focused and relatively strong plan to cover. It may take more time than you expected so do not give up once you have things moving in the right direction. It is very easy to go back to focusing on existing customers 100 percent of the time, and this happens very often. This is also why these programs must have top management sponsorship and support or they will drop to the side of the road.

We had a schedule to meet one of our more challenging customers for dinner. The sales manager had invited me along, and we were going to prepare for the dinner an hour before we left the hotel. We met in the lobby, and before I knew it, we were viewing a full-scale sale presentation that would be discussed at dinner. I asked a few questions of which one was, "what is the customer expecting to talk about tonight." They told me they had already told the customer we would be discussing a major promotion in detail. I then asked how the customer reacted and was told he seemed to be okay with it but did not have any real comments at the time. He was interested and looking forward to meeting our sales management but had no expectations or needs. After letting the team go on for a bit longer, I suggested an idea. What if we were not to talk at all about our sales promotion but get to know each other better (since there were a few new people) and see where the evening leads us? Through the years I have been with many customers who, after working all day, might just want to take time to relax and build the personal relationships at a dinner like this. I also brought up the fact that if the customer wants to discuss business, he will most likely bring it up. I could see some confusion on their faces as they did not want to argue about this but they were concerned about how they would get the promotion information to the customer as this was the time they had set aside. We talked about the situation and by all means if the customer wants to discuss the promotion then to do it. Another strategy would be to just generalize the program and send him the details later. This would prevent us from having to drag paperwork and computers with PowerPoint out at the restaurant. I also knew we were not scheduled to leave the next day and had some time just in case we could get an invite to his office.

We agreed to try this and were off to dinner. It was an enjoyable time, and the salesperson responsible for the account did a great job just having everyone interact. The customer did not want to talk about the promotion in depth so we gave him the high-level review. In general, he liked what we were proposing. We then dropped the business conversation and went back to enjoying our dinner. Toward the end of the dinner, he said he enjoyed the relaxing evening and wondered if we had time to stop by the next morning to go into detail about the program.

Now, this does not happen all the time and some customers just always want to talk business. The relationship with these customers, I realized over time, is a bit shakier as you never get to really know them well other than from a business climate. I found that my most loyal customers were the ones who took the time to get to know more about our company and our people than just the product offerings. This again is not 100 percent of all customers as some just do not want to cross the business/personal line. This did not stop me from calling on them even though I did have more of a complete relationship with the ones that wanted to do more than business 100 percent of the time.

I told each of my customers, usually early on, that they should "want" to get to know me. I normally got twenty-plus calls a day and who did they think I called back first? I had many choices to make each week, and I made choices for the people I knew the best first. This is human nature, and I always wanted to take care of all my customers, just maybe the ones I was closest to received priority.

This again goes for all company management. When getting to see customers, try to get to know them a bit. Do not be afraid to ask them what they like to do and how their weekend went. You can find out a lot about people in a short time. A large part of business is doing it with people you like, and customers have that same feeling. When proposing your solution and all things are close to equal, I guarantee the person closest to the customer in a broadened relationship has the edge. When we had the closest relationship and the right solution, we always felt we had the best chance to win an order. This is not doing anything unethical at all. This is just plain good business, and a sales team is expected and paid to have this type of situation in place. I could always rely on my best salespeople to have a relationship with our customers that would allow us the opportunity to win. You should expect the same from any sales team you assemble if you are to be successful. There is one other important point that is not discussed very often. A close relationship with a customer also gets you honest feedback quicker. I have had customers tell me to ease off as my offering just is not the right fit. This is a high level of respect the customer has for a salesperson. They do not want them to waste any more time on promoting something that the customer will not buy from them. Many customers just will not tell this information to a salesperson for many reasons. When they begin to share this with a salesperson, then the relationship has risen to a very high level with a customer that will lead to many orders as time goes on.

Building a strong channel strategy focused on mutual loyalty will harvest year over year revenue growth.

Chapter 5

Managing Different Channels to the Market

There are agents, representatives, distributors, telemarketers, Web sites, storefronts, direct and many other more ways to promote your products to the general marketplace. Since the Web site is a well-known means and widely used in many companies today, I will focus more on the human relationship element. This is a large piece of the other means listed above in selling your products. No matter what way you decide to promote your products, it is inevitable that you will, at some time, have to interact with a channel to your customer or your customer directly. Since we have already discussed the customer in a previous chapter, I will focus on a very important and at times critical interface to your customer. The *end customer* is defined as "the one who purchases your offerings." Companies usually have some type of mix as to how they sell their products. Many times this is some percent of direct complemented by some type of channel to the market. Many companies use channels for a number of reasons:

1. The cost of setting up a logistic team for a manufacturer to coordinate the many things associated with dealing directly to a customer is many times difficult to justify.
2. The business world is set up into many complicated geographic conditions. Historically, many customers buy from a local source. This is based on service and special skills, such as contracting, design, or twenty-four-hour support to name a few.

3. Technical assistance on choosing the right product for the right application. With the numerous products available in the market many times it is difficult for a customer to select the right product for their application. Many times no one manufacturer has it all, so the local source can assist in selecting the product combinations best suited for a project.

I could name more, but hopefully, you already know why your company has a particular channel strategy. If you do not understand why you have a chosen channel to your customer, I suggest you quickly sit down with your company management and figure it out. My background has always been a mixture of a channel business and customer direct. At the companies I was associated with, I found the direct business was always a small percentage of the overall sales revenue for the companies I worked for. This gave me a chance to work with many great channel companies in finding ways to promote products to our customers. Going direct and engaging in the entire sales fulfillment process with a customer throws a large burden on a manufacturing company. It requires large customer service and support teams. It may require a dedicated outside salesperson for each direct customer account. This is not to say that there is not a place for a direct sales strategy; it is just from my experience it is best to keep this with a focused and very specialized team.

Let me define a few different channels that can be used in the general market and the reason they are successful in what they do. Some of these channels are used as your direct sales team while others work with your corporate team. There are times when both situations occur within a company's market strategies.

Distributors normally run a local or regional business. These are in the industrial, commercial, retail, and many other sectors. I am grouping them all together as the model is similar as are the tools to manage them from a sales perspective. In a few select industries there are national distributors or chains as they are sometimes called. You will find many local distributors survive very well, sometimes even when competing with a larger distributor, as customers have come to value their expertise. These companies buy direct from the manufacturers and have stock of many different products to fit their market needs, at their locations. They have formal agreements with select manufacturers and sell at a market price to their customers. The customer goes to them for support but can also go directly to the manufacturers if needed. Some distributors live on product sales margins only while the trend has been to expand services to find other ways of assisting customers to bring in additional revenue. Distributors usually have a representative directly assigned to them from the manufacturers they have agreements with. These are the manufacturers salespeople we discussed earlier in the book. It is key that these salespeople are freed up to spend as much time as possible working with their distributors.

Agents and representatives are normally people chosen by a manufacturer to complement an existing corporate sales force or be that sales force. For some manufacturers, it is expensive and often difficult to put in place a sales force to cover all areas so agents or representatives have been key in assisting manufacturers in their growth. They have expertise in certain aspects of the industry and usually have business and personal relationships with key customers. They represent numerous lines of products and are normally paid on a percentage commission on a scheduled basis. They sometimes stock a small amount of product even though they work with distributors similar to a direct salesperson. Many companies use these types of organizations to help get started and then, if necessary, move to a direct sales team. Even saying this, many manufacturers are very successful staying with these type of channels over the long term. In a later chapter, I will discuss telemarketing and inside sales. These are different and both are strong ways to obtain additional sales when utilized correctly.

Since this is not a book on distribution marketing and sales, I have definitely oversimplified the types of channels detailed above. I also know there are many types and combinations of ways to the market even within these channel organizations. Over the years, they have become a large part of the industry they serve. They should be held in high respect as a key component in a successful sales and support strategy. They will add a layer of information about the market, which usually cannot be attained by a manufacturer's sales team. They have a unique style and relationship with customers. This customer relationship is difficult to explain and often complicated to understand, so this is why manufacturers should strengthen their relationships with their channels. Even when some customers demand a direct manufacturer relationship in their operations, many customers still work closely and purchase many daily items from their channel organizations. These channels normally complement and interact closely with a manufacturer's sales team, and as stated previously, the agent or representative channel may also be viewed as the manufacturer's sales team in certain situations.

I made the mistake when I was heading up sales for a small industrial computer company. I came in and quickly set up my own sales team, which was costly to do. I did not give the representatives in the market, who were selling and representing our product, enough attention to understand their value. Nor did I spend enough time reviewing the financials. We were paying a percentage to our reps, and as I brought on salespeople directly reporting to me, the costs went up and the revenues failed to follow. I tell this story because there is not just one model in the marketplace to follow when setting your sales strategy. I would suggest very focused and ongoing review of selling costs and performance. I did not say *time-consuming* and *overcomplicated*; I said *focused*. Look at your situation periodically with an eye on any changes in the market. I learned this the hard way because I did not take the time to understand market particulars. I hope this advice will help you to take time to make sure you look at different ways to set up your sales organization and market channels and not get hung up on just one. I learned a valuable lesson that helped me do a much better job in this area as I moved into other situations when it came to setting up sales organizations and market support teams.

We were summoned to a customer meeting, and the agenda was simple. The new procurement person wanted to reduce costs. They had decided that to do this, it was best to have their main product manufacturers come in and discuss a plan to allow them to buy directly. They appreciated the local distributor, but wanted to cut out what they viewed as a percentage of profit the distributor was getting for supplying them their products. We were familiar with most of the people at the meeting as we arrived and were introduced to the new procurement manager. I never liked new people as they have a tendency to rush right into their agenda and never take time to understand current process or participants. The comparison to these people, whenever I was in this situation, is similar to a railroad locomotive. There was no time to review history; it was just right to the subject of how they could start to buy directly and cut the middleman out. Of course, you could see the other people, in the customer company, cringe when this was brought up even though they knew it was the main subject. Their eyes looked at us, and you could see they were hoping we had some good counter-offer that would save the distributor whom they needed to obtain the products and support from each day.

We started to explain the benefits of distribution to all participants. We reviewed the support and local stock benefits as well as their local service 24/7. Looking into the eyes of the procurement manager, you could sense he was not interested in this conversation even though he was giving us the stage at the moment. It was time to tell them that buying direct increases our, the manufacturer's, costs. We would have to add logistical people while we were also not set up to do billing and all the other functions contributing to selling and supporting multiple locations and ordering small quantities of multiple orders daily. We also pointed out customers have critical daily needs that we find are better served by the local distributor who is set up just for this reason.

Well, as you can guess, things were not going very well and we were running out of supporting evidence as to why they should continue to do business as they were presently. We had to get the real issue on the table as there was conflict with what this manager wanted us to do for him. We knew this procurement manager and his team had to come out of this meeting with a win, and it was very evident that win was directly associated with some type of price concession. Our win was to minimize the price concession, but more importantly, we had to keep our distributor in the equation. It was critical the distributor keep supporting the customers' internal and external teams, especially the ones at this meeting. They all relied on the distributor to keep the operations going on a daily basis, and it would be very difficult as a manufacturer to come close to fulfilling this requirement.

Well, it was time to offer a compromise. We would negotiate directly with the procurement team and anyone else in their company to put together an annual pricing and support agreement. This included product types, quantities, and price discount levels. We also offered to look at a rebate program based on volume that would be established annually by both parties. The customer would then be able to have direct contract with us that would give them preferred agreements while still being able to work daily with the local distributor. If they demanded from us, they could buy direct, but we took a strong stance that our direct price and the price they buy from our distributor would be the same. We supported this by going back to our discussion on doing the total order fulfillment process. We offered to host a management annual review meeting to evaluate the progress of this proposal and it would be the customer's choice as to who would be in attendance. At this meeting, we could also adjust and make changes if needed.

It worked and all parties were happy. We came into the meeting knowing we would have to compromise in some areas and were prepared to do this. We also knew the customer had additional business to give us if we could just put a program together that would open up those opportunities. More importantly, our contacts at the company, who made their operations perform, were relieved they could still deal with their key suppliers.

It is imperative that a manufacturing company has a defined and understood channel policy. If the policy is weak, then people inside the manufacturer will deem it upon themselves to interpret or define what they believe the policy should be. This causes confusion with the manufacturer's sales team (who absolutely must know the policy) and more importantly, the customer and the channels. Understand, communicate, and firmly enforce your channel policy. When you do, you will see sales increase through this group as they will support your company with total engagement of your strategies.

This is not an uncommon occurrence in everyday business. Sometimes it is on a smaller scale. Companies you work with want to know they are getting a good deal, and the sales team must find ways to convey this. The key to getting this type of program in place is to give your sales team and the channels you associate with full support once the strategies are in place. Company management should expect each sales team to prepare a simple review on each distributor in their territory. This review should include strategies on how to keep, increase, and expand business. A well-prepared sales team works closely with their channels to grow customer business. They meet on a regular basis and must expect each other to be open and frank on all matters. It takes a major effort to obtain a customer, and when accomplishing this with a channel associate, the manufacturer will see their business increase in other areas also. This is the result of the channel company focusing more time on selling a manufacturers' product line they feel more committed to.

For companies that do a majority of their business through a channel of some type, this channel must be included in business planning sessions as they normally bring in a valuable local view which manufacturers tend to lack. Sitting down with a channel company and reviewing their territory customers to lay out simple-to-execute sales tactics for customers is essential to the relationship. Channels companies value this type of opportunity, and it also gives the manufacturers an opportunity to meet and build relations with the channels management. Meeting up with channel companies at trade shows or other events does not allow quality time to really understand each other. Top management, especially sales management, should have one key strategy for their channels companies, which includes growing the customer base together. Get to know channels as much as possible on a one-to-one basis. It is easy to see top channel management in group settings, but is more important to engage them one-on-one. Manufacturers must travel to the channel home office to encourage this interaction. When they do this, they will gain respect from not only the channel as a whole but also their own field sales team. I suggest any manufacturer to implement a travel schedule to customers and channel companies on a regular basis for their key management team. They would also be wise to request support of key programs when meeting with channel management. I also told my sales teams not to be shy about asking what type of profit margin the channel needed to run a successful business. It was also a good practice to compare how you as manufacturer stacked up with other companies in this area. There is nothing wrong with asking how your company rates in channel profits compared to all the other companies they deal with. This is also very valuable information to bring back to your management as it is key to be viewed by the channel management as a profitable manufacturer to work with. It also gives a salesperson some leverage as to what type of effort to expect from a given channel company. Sales volumes and profits are the key to encouraging any business to support your programs, and you should expect your channel businesses to give you the support equal to your contributions. Remember, most channels have multiple product lines they support, so the key is to get as much of their attention as possible. The closer you are and the more attention you give to them, the more you will receive. I have seen many manufacturing companies approach a channel company with exotic business plans. They are filled out in detail and then fall to the wayside. These companies have many manufacturers to support, and they will extend extra effort with the ones that create an environment that is simple to work in. If you just sit down and do basic customer and promotion planning laid out in easy tactics and reporting, you will get more time from the channel team. Make it simple, and success will come.

Channel councils are another area that always amused me. It is a great opportunity to put some real issues on the table, yet many times these group sessions are wasted. The problem with most councils is getting real issues on the discussion agenda! There are all types of mundane issues, such as a mislabeled box, a wrong invoice, and a product lacking one feature that causes it not to sell. Not that these are not issues; it is just that channel councils are not the place to bring them up. It seems that many companies want to have some type of third-party council or committee to get feedback and solve problems. One glaring problem is the lack of preparing the group for a productive meeting so their feedback is weak and normally they do not have the right people in the meeting. After many years of being part of these sessions, I came up with a method to really get some things accomplished.

These are some of the items I suggest you do if you really want to obtain results from these type channel council of sessions:

1. Take time to really select the right members from both sides. This is not very hard if you focus on key people that have an open mind and are willing to represent what is good for the whole. The channel council must be made up of somewhat equal geography, and the members should be comfortable and have a base relationship with the manufacturing management. You do not need or want a player who is

always negative, wants to take on small issues affecting only a few, or is just trying to get political visibility. From the manufacturers' side, they must choose key sales group people, marketing people who have decision-making capability, operations and possibly a finance person. The people chosen must understand that these sessions are not the time to make a defensive stance or get offended by anything said by anyone. It is not a time to specifically have answers for many items discussed, but a time to take input, clarify the issue or opportunity and then take it back for more review. Some people just cannot resist getting into a conflict be it the channel or the manufacture members. This meeting strategies must be clarified before the parties meet, and the rules of engagement must be set at the opening of the meeting.

2. Send out a detailed agenda a week beforehand and ask for additional subjects to be added. Assign homework to both parties if some fact-finding is needed so you can have this at the meeting. Make sure the items on the agenda are real items and not just some unwarranted subject that does not justify attention. If any item comes back from the channel group that is not appropriate, call and tell them this will be taken care of in a different way. The best way to finalize the agenda is to assemble a small team from the manufacturer that is not political to finalize.

3. Start with an evening before kicking off dinner. Make this informal, and end the dinner with a review of the next day's agenda. The next morning, go over what has been accomplished since the last meeting, introduce any new members, and remind everyone the rules of engagement in these meetings. Make sure you clarify that if anyone strays outside the rules of the meeting, the monitor will bring the meeting back on track. I find that one whole day is all you need to get the major items discussed and actions assigned. I also hope it is very apparent you must have a strong moderator who is not intimidated by anyone in the room and holds everyone on the same level.

4. Present each agenda item, and give the issue/opportunity time for discussion. Then close the item or assign action plans with timetables to someone at the meeting. I know this sounds so repetitive, but you

can then keep a simple spreadsheet of each item: who is responsible, what they need to do, and when. The moderator is responsible not to let the meeting go to the next agenda item if resolution or plans have not been completed for the one currently being discussed.

5. Conclude the meeting by setting a date to get the minutes and assigned items out to everyone. This should happen quickly so the channel members can send these out to their associates in their region. It is also necessary so that people assigned to work teams can move forward.

6. Do not allow yourself to have too many action items coming out of these meetings or you will be severely disappointed in the results. Also, do not allow one or two people to take all the actions on themselves. They will not complete them and then excuses will abound. Spread the workload and let everyone participate.

The post meeting's biggest challenge is to have that one person who has to have power in the company push open items to closure. Remember that when everyone leaves to go back to their work duties, they have a whole stack of tasks at hand. To keep priority on the council items, the assigned moderator must revisit them each week and establish contact with any assigned person who does not meet the agreed-upon time to complete their task. I found a personal visit or call was best and also publishing the items each two weeks would keep the pressure on people to complete what they promised to do. This is the number one failure of councils and many meetings. How many times do people go to the next session and most of the things promised from the last session are still open? If you really want a channel council to be successful, then stay on high-level issues/opportunities, get things done, and implement the improvement plans quickly. Do not let some other person or team second-guess what the council has deemed to be put in place. You will find there are many on both sides that will resist buying into change.

It is very important you must keep this simple and just let these councils get things done and done quickly. It is sometimes very easy to delay even the simplest action plans and just make excuses until they just go away. By keeping this to a simple spreadsheet item by item with as few details as possible, you will find actions are easier to follow and complete. Again, do not let one or two individuals take on too many tasks and make sure that the majority of any action items will be attainable within a two- to three-month period or at least before the next council meeting. Just keep it as simple as possible just like we have discussed throughout this book. A few last comments are to put emphasis on getting the most important things on the action list and then completing them before the next meeting takes place. Also, consider changing channel representatives every two years and overlap these changes so you get 20-25 percent new people six months or so. I also would not allow a channel company to attend these unless the owner or the number two person in their company has committed to be on the team. Do not allow a low-level person to be part of any council; if the channel does not want to send a high official, then the council is not important to them.

These channel councils and the results from them can be a very powerful way to increase revenues for all involved. As a manufacturer, by getting your sales team and channel companies going in the same direction, there is tremendous energy focused on selected strategies. If you really want to unleash the power of your whole sales arsenal, then set these sessions up, select some critical programs you need to move forward, make sure you have everyone associated with these programs in line, and unleash them to perform.

Focused inside sales teams are a stealth weapon which when used properly create key additional sales revenues

Chapter 6

The Power of Inside Sales Teams

I t took me years to fully understand the power of a well defined inside sales team. I knew they were always busy and also were very helpful in many areas related to customer support. What it took me a while to comprehend is their powerful impact on company sales revenues. Many companies define their inside sales team as a mixture of many job descriptions. These commonly are customer service, technical support, telemarketing, and at times, administration. I am sure if you ask a typical inside salesperson what they do, they could add to this list. So what am I trying to get at? I am going to define and lay out what could be the most powerful team you have in your company when it comes to assisting customers, backing up and making your outside sales team more affective, and being a key part of increasing sales revenues. You probably have some type of current inside on-the-phone sales/customer support team. What I suggest to a company is to first really look at what they have in-house currently and define what your inside teams' responsibilities are. This is not to say that you currently have a defined inside sales team as it could be called something different. As I define what an inside sales team does, I hope you will understand the power of this team and realize you would never do business again without a group like this.

I do not feel the need to define customer service, telemarketing, or technical support that I alluded to previously. What I will do is define the responsibilities and how to engage a productive and focused inside sales team. The responsibilities or job descriptions in general are as follows:

- Focus on presales activities only (this is key) that ultimately will bring in more orders.
- Work closely with assigned outside sales personnel in generating more sales in their assigned territory.
- Work closely with assigned channels on presale programs that are currently being promoted by the company.
- Be available by phone or e-mail to customers who have preorder questions whether technical or commercial.
- Work closely with the marketing teams to assure correct rollout of company promotions and major programs.
- Assist the outside sales team in managing their sales opportunity sheet by assisting them in bringing potential orders to a close.

These are just a few, and key to this group is to emphasize the focus of this team in the presale area. There are many programs that occur within a company at any given time, and these are many times assigned to the territory outside salespeople to implement. With the complicated world and the added responsibilities, it is very difficult for any one salesperson to keep all the balls in the air. It is frustrating to marketing teams when they feel the support they need for a given program is not fully there. I think I have made my point now; if you are buying in on this, let me continue.

I went into the management review meeting to propose some changes in the organization. I was not asking for more people but just a rearrangement of responsibilities to put them where they belonged. I presented the fact that we were not benefiting from the new marketing programs as well as we could and that these programs were in need of more focus. Of course, the outside sales team and channels were always taking the blame when the new promotions fell short of expectations. I took the initiative to attempt to define what type of effort it would take to get these programs up and running. Once a selected promotion gets off the ground, it is then much easier to assign this to the field sales team and channels in the field. Some promotions are just not going to get the visibility from the field sales teams and they must get jump-started from another source within the company. They also need to be fine-tuned once a good factual feedback chain is established.

I could start to see the interest in the faces of the marketing people present at the meeting as this situation was very important to them and the company management. I stated we had a few people dedicated to phone support to assist the sales and channel teams. They were doing all the things that were asked of them, buy pre-sales activities were basically low on the scale, if at all. The marketing department had them doing telemarketing with a very low rate of success. They were also assigned a mixture of expediting, correcting orders, taking quality-and-product issue questions. This was just a small example of why, when the day was completed, this team was exhausted, confused, de-motivated, and overloaded with tasks to accomplish. They had, as they told me frequently, too many different tasks to accomplish in a given day. They wanted to do a few things successfully rather than do many unsuccessfully. This is when I went into what we really needed to fulfill: the presale tasks that are currently falling short of our expectations. What we needed was a focused pre-sales team to get things off the ground. I said if we would just divert a few people who were doing multiple tasks to a pre-sale focused group, they would be the ones to promote selected company promotions and be responsible to get them off and moving in a positive direction. We laid out a detailed job description similar to the general one I previously showed. I suggested we give this team a chance and apply measurement to their progress. There was an air of confusion in the room. As I looked around, it was not really disagreement but just a feeling of "Okay, but how does this really work?" We assembled a team dedicated to just this!

This could be your current situation if you do not have a true inside sales team. The education of internal and external people associated with what you will be trying to do is very difficult. You need to start with a marketing team and challenge them to give you a few programs they needed done in the pre-sales area. They usually come back with a promotion that is just not going anywhere. The next step is to break off a few good inside people and set your team up. They need to take on the marketing promotions follow up on calling channel companies and getting them to place orders for a stated promotion package on a new product line. In the case above, we went after the promotion that was just dead in the water and within a month, the results were outstanding. We again kept it simple and did not bog down the inside team with a lot of reporting other than results on getting orders or commitments for orders. By the way, we also had formed a compensation package that rewarded these inside people with a commission on a monthly basis. This was important to do monthly so they could celebrate in their success and see the results in their pockets quickly. This does keep the enthusiasm up as, remember, the people whom you assign this job should have the drive like any other typical good salespeople. I would suggest not just choosing someone from customer service or another area to fill these spots unless they have a sales-driven mentality. It is too easy to assign just a few people to do this without looking for the correct personalities. If you just move some people into this position without a sales drive then you are doomed for failure.

As time goes on and this concept settles in, there is a tendency to give them, this team, too many tasks. This is why a company must have a strong manager in place so someone can keep the focus on the high-priority assignments. The review of results and the next programs for this sales team must be discussed frequently. Sales, marketing, and company management must decide what the most critical programs for this team are and how to measure results. Some programs are just not going to go anywhere, and there comes a time where they must be cut out. It is important to realize when it is time to change the assignments and allow the team to move into the next challenge. Without a focused timely review of programs progress, this team can become unproductive and de-motivated. To reiterate, the manager of this team must be able to stand up to any management challenges and also be capable of determining when a project the team is working on is completed or should be replaced with another.

So now, we had some momentum from inside the company to utilize this team in the correct fashion. The other side of the challenge was educating the outside environment in order to get and give this inside team air cover so they could do their job. Typically people call people who get the job done for them. We are all very tired of the voicemail rollercoaster we have in our world today. Most people try to bypass this and go directly to the "person" who can help them. This is golden to many; as everyone has to much to do and not enough time to do it. People want answers quickly, and the stress builds the longer they have to wait. You have to educate the companies you support as to who to call for what then make sure your internal teams follow the guidelines strictly. It is difficult at first even to change the habits of people calling into the company for assistance. It is almost equally difficult to have a person who has been working with people they know to redirect a call they are no longer responsible for. Once this inside team redirects a call that they may have, in the past, answered themselves, the next person to pick up this call must satisfy the caller. As natural as it is to have a "go to" person in a company, it is the same when getting an answer for a person whom you have been helping for a period of time. It is very difficult to break these habits especially if it is viewed as being a successful way that has worked in the past. For some time, the calls into people will continue the same even from your own sales team. The people taking the calls must be politely firm as to the changes and route the calls to correct areas within the company. If this does not happen, then any presales activities assigned to the inside sales will not be nearly as effective as they should be. They must have high focus on presales programs assigned to them and meet their assigned goals with no excuses, especially "too much other work" type of excuses. The manager of this team must keep a close eye on this process in the early stages to break the habits of the past. I assure you this inside team is a hidden weapon that every company should consider. It complements the outside team by assisting them in organizing their territory plans while also completing critical company promotions that many times do not get full attention from the sales team and then fall short of expectations.

To monitor this team, a simple spreadsheet of the activities is suggested and needed with metrics assigned and a timetable with definitions of what equals success for a given set of activities. Such programs as getting a new promotion off the ground is sometimes just delivered through the mail, e-mail, or a phone call explaining and reviewing the details. I was constantly frustrated by the amount of promotions being thrown at the field sales team. Monthly, there was always the claim that some of these were not receiving the correct attention from the sales group. With all the activities taking place in the field, there is always a handful of activities that do not get the attention required to get them off and moving. This is easy to if you review the spreadsheets with the activities and results of these programs. So how did we attack this situation? We decided to assign the most critical promotions to the inside sales team. We took a spreadsheet and listed the responsibilities such as who would call who, what was the message, and then the timetable to get the commitment. The results were outstanding as we now had a focused team pre-selling a selected promotion in an exclusive manner. We would review every few days, and with this type of focus, the team was literally forced to meet the goals. They met their goals and this launched the future of how marketing would set up their promotions with the sales group for selected promotions. The other interesting outcome of this was the scheduling of promotions. Of course, the marketing teams are always vying for sales time in some area of getting their products to be accepted and revenues generated. We began to have a whole different relationship with the marketing teams. The inside sales manager would meet on a scheduled basis and lay out the timetable for promotions from all the marketing groups. What also came out of this was the discipline that if you wanted something done by the inside sales team, then you needed to be sensitive to the timing and not just "throw it over the fence." This does not mean we did not have to deal with emergencies that might come out of top management needs. The key is to stay strong, and when emergencies do occur, they were given immediate attention and closed out as quickly as possible.

I want to emphasize again that this is not a telemarketing team and should never be used for that purpose. This team should be focused on presales revenue-generating high-percentage-success activities. This is not cold calling or discovery-type work. This is focused on existing customers and channels in the market you are associated with. These people should be given a certain level of authority to make common decisions, and this will make the programs they deal with successful. Once you get someone on the phone, the promotion needs to be driven to closure as you need to move on to the next opportunity. Many companies waste valuable time with low percentage of success in trying to generate new business with unknown customers. By focusing on relations you already have, results can happen quickly. There is no time in this type of inside team setup to labor people with massive reports or tasks that take them away from focusing on what is really important. By keeping it simple and focused, this inside sales team will be one of the most successful groups a company can assemble in today's business environment.

Measurements based on anything but bringing in orders are a waste for any sales team

Chapter 7

Measuring the Productivity
of Your Sales Teams

E very sale team must be challenged to meet and beat the company revenue plans. This must be natural, and it must come from the sales management and be delivered very clearly to the rest of the team. The environment this creates is one of unity within the sales team and respect from the overall company employees. There is nothing worse than a mediocre sales team and its sales management. A strong and qualified sales team must be continually challenged as they are willing and ready to respond. If members of a sales team moan and complain about new challenges, then a company must make changes. When you recruit and hire the best salespeople, they will exceed your expectations continually. A sales management team that is known for excuses as to why they did not "bring in the orders" is also not seen as strong leaders to their own sales team. Think of the sales force as line troops for the company who must take the charge to make the whole company strong. The leader is key to motivating this team to exceed all expectations.

We were informed our company had just announced another merger. We were the primary company and had acquired another that was a niche in the industry. The products and services would definitely complement ours, and everyone was very positive. We were called into the merger-planning meeting and, of course, assigned tasks. As always, one of the most emotional and probably the most important task was to decide how to bring the two organizations together. As usual, one of the first topics was, how many people do we need to support the new company and then how do we decide whom to let go? I have had to do this numerous times and my best suggestion is to start by looking as closely as possible to sales productivity measurements, keep the emotional part to a minimum. This was going through my mind as we all left the room to our separate conference rooms to begin the evaluation. What happened next was typical in that the managers from the newly merged company wanted to give opinions of their people. This is always the typical way to start, and is one piece of the puzzle to ultimately find out who was on the "bubble" so to say. Luckily, I had been through many of these mergers so the best thing to do is just relax, sit back, and give full attention. It helps the process if the two companies' management are aware of their future status and if they will have roles in the new organization. This typically leads one of two attitudes, non-engagement or cooperative interest. In this current situation, I let the talking go on for many hours and took notes. That night over dinner the same conversation kept going, and we started to talk about measurements and how productive certain people were. Productivity comes in different forms, and as you know from previous chapters, my number one criteria is sales revenue results and growth in a salesperson's assigned territory. In this situation, it was quickly obvious that the other management team had many other types of criteria of which many had nothing to do with sales revenue performance. They told me about the top players and how well they filled out weekly sales reports. They were never late with reports and always had a thorough explanation if sales were not meeting their assigned goals. Others were very good at managing their budget and always were very detailed on their expenses. Some of their top performers in ratings were the best at controlling their spending and were always under their expense budgets. It also seemed the same names came up as to the most cooperative with management, never bringing up any problems with the business strategies. Well, it was time to adjourn and get ready to meet the next morning.

We all met with fresh coffee in hand (pastries also even though they do not seem to go well with our slimmed-down culture anymore), and it was our turn to ask questions as we had been listening for hours the day before. The following are some of the questions we asked:

1. Let us see the sales revenue results versus plan over the past years for each person and territory.
2. Have there been any changes that would have weighted a territory so a person could have been given a windfall sales order/orders typically called a "blue bird"?
3. Size of each salesperson's territory and perceived market share currently attained.
4. Sample report on customers in the territories and the previous two years' sales volume numbers broken down into selected product lines.
5. Results obtained from the past two to three company marketing promotions as it relates to the channels acceptance and successes.

Some of this was readily available, and we began to look it over. By this time, I was getting a better feel as to who I could possibly trust and get honest feedback from so now was the time to break off and start evaluating the above data with a smaller group. Even though this sounds a bit quick to start breaking the group up, this is the right thing to do. It is fairly easy, once you do this a few times, you can quickly spot the people who really want to make this process productive. Typically in a merger, the time frame for initial feedback to the company is short so you must get some decisions made. The risk of delaying some type of initial or preliminary plan is that some other merger manager will start to take control and make decisions for your team.

The next step was to bring back the entire group the next day to discuss our findings in more detail. I have found that usually you do not have to protect any current salesperson from either company if the results they are achieving are in line with expectations. There are times when circumstances do affect sales revenue results, and these need to be taken into consideration. This is why you need to look at a longer time to see what the trend has been for a particular territory or salesperson. It is very difficult to come up with any conclusions, positive or negative, by reviewing a short time span while an expanded time frame really helps to clarify the situation. In this case, we reviewed what we had and found some normal commonalities related to the sales industry. The salespeople who were good at budgets and reports, in general, always positive feedback (possible politicians) were not the ones on top of the revenue and sales results list. This never surprises me especially when it was obvious the management deemed this to be a large part of measuring success for their sales team members. I have found your sales team will change their behavior to meet the management expectations. Mine were always "get more orders" so we always beat our goals. In this case these people were also in the lower category for their distributors' selling and promoting the new product lines. We also made a few calls to the merging company's VP levels in other departments and found the people they listed, as not assisting in resolving issues, were the same people on our list of concern. It never hurts to go outside the sales management team of the company you are merging with to get comments on people you are evaluating. We found these same salespeople had a reputation to accept what they were told and then not come back with new ideas for improvement; they just had a tendency to give up. It became apparent quickly who the sales team top players were. This normally is fairly easy given the criteria listed previously. The real hard part is getting that next tier of people who might be new to the sales team, in a tougher territory, and not getting results just yet or was just a hidden winner who has not yet been given the right chances. We looked over even more information on this group and again asked others in the company for their opinions. We then made more decisions and suggested the list of people that would not make the cut.

It was now time to present our results and recommendations to the management team. As usual, many questions were asked and we answered them to the best of our ability and used the information we had for back up. I then met separately with some of the top management to get their reading on just how many people we would be allowed to keep. I found through doing this many times in my career that this periodically changes, especially since all departments are working on their teams also. At times, one group must cut deeper than others in order to save critical people for the organization. This is where real teamwork comes into play, and the company can grow stronger if all people come to the table with the attitude of doing the best things for the whole company. We adjourned for another evening then to give the recommendations one more night of thought. I was on the phone that night a few more times then the next morning we had another management meeting to finalize the teams and set an action plan into place. I presented my teams' final recommendations and met with the top management to finalize the direction and timetable we would take. It is always best to get this whole organization strategy completed and announced as quickly as possible. There is basically minimal work being done as emotions are high and everyone is waiting for the company's announcements. We went to work on the phone and in person, and in seven days, it was completed and people knew where they stood. Whether it was good or bad, it was done and done quickly.

Combining teams in a merger situation quickly and professionally shows respect for all the people involved even if the news to some is not what they wanted to hear. By delaying announcements of known organizational changes, you encourage rumors and leaks which will happen very fast. It is the management's responsibility to minimize the opportunity for people to start rumors, which cause massive confusion and setbacks in moving forward with the new organization. You do risk mistakes being made with some individuals; both the ones you keep as well as let go. I have found this is usually minimal when you do your evaluations in detail and with as many categories as possible to make the overall picture clear. I have seen disasters occur when a company waits too long to make decisions and basically beat the process to death. Get it done and move on as fast as possible is my recommendation.

The reason I took the time to tell this story was twofold. One was to hopefully assist those who have never been through an organization change and make the process successful. The other point is even more important: set a productivity measurement program in place to assure the company management teams the correct measurements are in place that deliver expected results. I have always been amused by people inside and outside of a sales group discussing productivity measurements for a sales team. I suggest keeping it simple, but again, it gets back to people who have not been in sales trying to measure salespeople as they do in other departments within the company. Can you imagine sales management setting productivity measurements for finance?

Now, that would be an interesting list, and I guarantee it would not fit the need. I would occasionally joke with my sales team that they could play golf every day as long as they were getting the sales revenues expected from their territory. Of course, I know this would not happen, but the point is that the number one item for them to focus on was meeting and beating their assigned sales quotas. I have fought many battles with company management on reports and held firm on my opinion on what was really needed. The reason again was to make sure we measured sales team performance on the most important criteria related to meeting and beating sales revenue goals.

An example of a report that is needed but should be left to the individual salesperson is a customer management system. Whether it is available software packages, which there are many, or just simple homegrown Word/Excel programs, they all work and they need to be simple. I remember times when someone would walk in and ask me to get the customer details for them so they could review it to see how the salesperson was doing. I always accommodated them and would also always follow up with them in a few days. The large majority of the time they failed to open it up to read or if they did read it, they came up with nothing that was beneficial other than a mailing list. I suggested if they really want to get to know the customer and how our sales team managed their customer base, they should get out and travel in the field on a scheduled basis. My belief is that up-to-date customers' data should be available to anyone in the company. This is expected, and if a salesperson does not have this type of information, then you do have a major problem. I just do not believe anyone should have to encourage a salesperson to keep an customer management database, they should have it automatically. The point is this is just one example of information that is important but of minor relevance when it comes to productivity measurements of a salesperson. I know if you are reading this it is causing some disagreement especially from a micro-manager type of person. I emphasize time and again to make sure you sit down and really understand what you want from your sales team. I will challenge anyone when it comes to having the sales team do anything that takes time away from them focusing the very large majority of their time on selling activities. This also again includes extensive paperwork and forms that ask for information that no one has time to respond to.

To this day, I always ask people in business how their sales team is measured and what the most important criteria in these measurements is. Another example is a salesperson's time management and should a company manage this as it is different for each situation. Some companies I know have implemented time management forms they require the sales team to complete. Of course, as usual, no one really reviews these consistently, and I emphasize *really*, even though many people will talk about how important they are to have. I just never understood why a salesperson had to fill out a form on what they were doing and what the results were. I just plain ask them, "When do you make up your weekly planning schedule?" If they tell me Monday morning of the current week, then it is time for me to coach them in another direction. Top salespeople have the next week or two planned ahead of the current week. Of course, there are always emergencies and cancellations, but the key is to be constantly thinking about next week and beyond. If I found a salesperson continuing to plan for the week on the current Monday morning, they would not last long in my organization.

We discussed channels to market in an earlier chapter, and productivity measurements must be a key part to this sales strategy. Keep it simple, and when reviewing business plans and revenue goals, make sure your sales team is held responsible to assure success with your channels. It is your sales team who must be held responsible to create and follow through with channels sales teams on their territory sales plans. This is also a good way to train them about the importance of keeping things simple so as not to muddy the water with items getting in the way of selling the company's products. Many times you can get into the habit of going down a path that ultimately turns into widely unrelated issues having nothing to do with getting orders. I found that making sure your company establishes the rules of how to build a simple sales plan and review process is much better than having your channels deliver theirs to you. When this is allowed to happen, you end up with many different reporting schemes which will use up many hours of your time to break down and understand. If you are smart, you will use the same type of reporting for your channels as you do for your sales team. By the way, the simpler you make the reporting requirements from your channels, the better they will do in getting them to you. Remember, they have their business to run, other manufacturers to report to, and they will welcome any assistance you give them to make their reporting more streamlined.

Create sales performance productivity measurements focused on what is important for your company to increase revenues, period! Keep them consistent, and refuse to add too many over time unless you eliminate an equal amount. Set time frames for review and make sure this continues to be a top priority for your sales management. By setting up this behavior, you will establish an environment focused on the channel and customer strategies you have established. Your company will also be viewed with respect in the industry of having a fair and simple method of dealing with your sales team and channels. Each industry is close nit and in every one I was associated with, I would at times, receive compliments on our policies and practices associated with our sales process from customers and channels. In fact, many times I was asked for advice from other non-competitive companies selling their products to our distributors regarding our policies. I remember golfing in an industry wide outing one year. I was approached by a VP sales from another competing company and he wanted to know about or car policy. It seems we had taken an industry leading role in offering an open policy that was the making our sales people very satisfied.

One thing good sales teams understand quickly is how they are being judged and what productivity measurements are important to the company. Once these have been established and reiterated over a period of time, the sales team understands what to focus on. Their reports will have very valuable information in them, and the review people will be able to focus on real areas for opportunities. The management team will have metrics which will assist them focusing on areas for improvement. The company will also understand customer concerns, which can be turned into opportunities. By making this simple, you have internal and external benefits, the internal we have discussed previously while the external will be getting the correct solutions for customers rapidly which outflanks the competition and wins more business. The ultimate outcome is getting your sales teams and channels into just selling more of your offerings.

I have had the opportunity of working with many great sales teams and people in my career. The stories I have will last a lifetime, and the real measurement of a great sales team is their focus and how they work together for a common goal. I would define this as a team that just focused solely on growing the business for the company. They take no prisoners and grow their customer and channel base by focusing only on the things needed to get orders. The sales revenue is always in the growth mode and normally in the double-digit percent. The outside and inside sales teams work very well with corporate marketing and it will show by all the successes you have in new company programs. The team is always willing to give the extra effort and is very aware and proud in their accomplishments. You will get off track a few times, and it is up to the entire team to realize this and get back on track. I remember one meeting when I was coming down pretty hard on the sales team for lack of focus on "just getting orders" when from the back door of the room, one of my new salesmen came in with a goofy mask on and made some just plain crazy statements. It shocked us all into a mode of just getting less serious about this whole thing and getting back to the basics of having fun and getting orders. The whole room went crazy and that was it; what else could I say but just shake my head. The next week, everyone was refreshed and we got back on track which resulted in a successful end to the year. I still believe the key was just defining in simple terms the performance requirements expected of them. In this case we got back to basics and focused on getting orders. Follow this technique and then sit back to enjoy the outcome.

Try a few new ideas and if you have the guts go for more

Chapter 8

Putting It All Together

I will now attempt to take the previous contents in this book and point out some key points to use when evaluating your present situation to see if your opportunities for improvement. Focus on simplifying the reports you require from your sales team, and focus on bringing in more sales revenue for the company. To accomplish this, I would emphasize the following areas:

- Review reporting structures and techniques. Really look at what you are trying to accomplish then streamline your program. Take this opportunity to set up a system that absolutely conveys to your company what the sales team should be doing.
- Find out what type of customer management tool your salespeople are using, and make sure it is not burdening them with doing things no one will ever use. Get your sales team focused on selling.
- Create a simple spreadsheet report for customer opportunities. Make this easy to use, and make it available so it can be used by different departments. Get a team of inner company personnel together to assist in forming the criteria on this sheet, remembering to focus on "what do we really need to help the sales team get more orders?"
- Establish and stick to timetables for review. Make it a priority, and make sure the right people are involved all the time. There should be no excuses to miss a meeting or conference call. In fact make the

meeting non-mandatory, and if people do not show up, this tells you there is a problem.

- Involve your IT team in this process, and get them to make this package easy to use and sort for data.
- Set up some simple guidelines as to what home office time should be used for. Put into play that the majority of home office time must be spent on customer and channel opportunities. Use this time for conference calls and training. Try to establish consistent time frames and days which the home office is available for other department calls. An example would be every Friday at 1:00 p.m. is new product training. Instruct departments within the company not to bother the sales team during the week when in the field "doing their selling stuff."

These are good starting points and these will start the process of stressing to your sales team the importance to the company of carving out more time to focus on selling.

This should now lead you into reviewing the sales compensation plan. You might decide you already have a great plan. If so, go ahead and get some of your sales team together and discuss it with them. The hard part here is that if your sales management team believes they have a good plan; it will be hard to get honest feedback from individual salespeople. They will discuss particulars they would like to see in their plan but normally only among themselves. Another way to go is to challenge your existing plan to see if it meets certain things that are proven to acquire, keep, and motivate a sales team.

Of course, if you are the boss and put together the current plan, then you must have thick skin and a strong staff open to improve your current program. Some things to focus on are as follows:

- A solid base pay package which can include a "secure" almost guarantee base pay each period. This is a key part.
- A commission or bonus plan also paid monthly or quarterly. This is based on meeting the sales revenue goals for a particular salesperson. This should be established at whatever time frame you desire, but do not deviate from the commission during the time frame established.

Once you are found to deviate for any reason, you will be doing it with more people more often. What I am trying to explain is if a salesperson is having a tough time because of some reason like the economy is bad right now, then get through it and work something in the next plan period. Do not react too quickly; changing any individual compensation plan will leak out to your entire team in days. By the way, do not be naïve and think it will not be known by all and brought up by many!

- Accelerated or expanded compensation when goals have been met and there is a company benefit to exceed the sales plan. To meet an annual goal, everything would have to be perfect and each salesperson would be at precisely 100 percent at year-end. This of course would be fantastic, but never realistic so you need to cover for the possibility that a few sales territories will not meet plan. Even if they all do, what is so wrong with beating the overall plan? An accelerated package goal should be focused on expanding opportunities to make sale over the assigned plan and then pay more than normal commissions for this amount. Do not be hesitant on this as I urge you to give it a try. As I stated previously, it will also assist you in defining who your top "go-getters" are in the field. Pay more for exceptional growth, and the company will see record results.

- To keep things exciting over the years, you may want to consider some type of timed incentives based on certain programs. I would steer away from "knee-jerk" monthly marketing or management compensation or reward programs. These tend to get into a "who can do better" game, and it detracts from your real focus. Do not let your company start to have your marketing team come up with a compensation program for every new promotion. You are paying your sales team a salary to support these, and they also get a commission to sell more. Remember, if you treat them like people who are just out for the next dollar, then you will sacrifice the professionalism to make them proud.

Any plan you establish should be unquestionably measurable. This cannot be compromised. Any commission or bonus plan has to be very tight so no one can say, "Well, this or that happened so let's just give them some extra money anyway." I have heard this time and again, and once the rules are bent you might as well be ready to do it again and again. Find other ways to react; if you find there is a very good reason to give some extra compensation to anyone, then figure it into the future plans for that individual and not as an immediate fix. Go ahead and explain this to the particular sales person so they understand the strategy behind your decision. They will have a stronger commitment to the company as they have been treated with the respect of a professional.

Once this is completed, share the basic ideas you have established with the people in the company who work with the sales team. The sales team must find ways to cooperate with others in the company. The people in the company already believe the salespeople make too much money, so why not show them how they make that money. I was always open to sharing the basic framework of the sales compensation plan with others as I would rather they know the facts than speculate all the time. When they see how the plan is designed and what the goals are, they will be more positive and less critical of the sales force. Also, encourage these same people to participate in the performance review meetings. By this I mean the weekly or monthly review of the spreadsheets on programs associated with customers or channels opportunities. Invite company management to be actively involved as they can assist in monitoring these meetings to bring a positive and productive atmosphere. This is the key time that you can nurture inner company relationships. There will still be some occasional disagreement; the key is to minimize this and get on with solutions to get more orders.

After you have set this in motion, it is time to direct everyone in the same direction and get this sales business moving forward. Start on the customer opportunity spreadsheet and begin training your team on how to fill it out. This is not hard, and people within the company need to be assigned to assist individual salespeople at the different stages of the sales process. Start by explaining the goals of the process. Have an initial meeting, and start to gather the "things we need to know to get orders" criteria, which will populate the spreadsheet. Dissect these down to the question of "is this really needed to bring in the purchase order?" When this is done then, finalize the sheet and have the kickoff meeting with the sales teams. Explain what their responsibilities are and set a date for the first meeting to review their territory opportunities. I suggest one week and then start the conference calls. If you have a salesperson who cannot fill in this simple sheet in one week, then you need to know this. By the way, that is one benefit of this program; if I had a salesperson who was struggling with this, then I knew we had a major problem with their focus. As this process continues, there will be tweaks and some additions to the opportunity sheet. Resist adding too much and continuously ask your team if the new addition does help get the order. You must stay on the course and continue to review this on a regular basis with everyone. Make timelines as to how long an opportunity is allowed to stay on the sheet. When time is up, move it to the side and add another. You can always bring back an opportunity; just do not let them sit on the sheet too long. I would always expect an opportunity to move forward in the sales process weekly and come to a close within three to four weeks. Remember, you are working on the "hot" opportunities. As this process continues and you include people from other departments, you will see the teams working closer together. One area you will have to watch closely are developments and promotions that are going nowhere. The team must be honest as to what the real problem is, and many times this is very difficult. You have a large group of people and when something is going wrong, it is usually someone's responsibility, they are on the hot seat. Lay it on the table then get everyone to acknowledge they will help the responsible person as that individual attempts to correct the situation. This goes both ways as the heat is also on the salesperson to close out the opportunity. The real winner in this program is the company, as these opportunities now get high-level attention which normally results in a higher hit rate for an order.

At some point, you should start on the channel sheet as it should also be reviewed and this should happen on a regional basis. The same format should be used to keep things consistent. So now you have sheets on the direct customer, channel customer, and channel programs/promotions opportunities for review. Channel management might be the next to implement this in their organization as they will be interested to know what their sales team is pursuing. This is a perfect time to get their "buy-in" on the program, and once you get this, then their sales team is under the gun to deliver you their opportunities. By now you can see the fantastic benefit of this whole process. The company can see the majority of business available at a given time; they have access to see the customer base and a time frame for getting a particular order. All people should be able to sort a selected opportunity quickly. What a powerful report to take to a review meeting, which I found most people were interested in reviewing to see if they could assist the sales team in any way.

In parallel with this, you can have your inside sales team create a sheet with the selected promotions they are planning to start work on. Detail it as you see fit, remembering the key is to have items on it only if it is needed to help get the order. This is one program that will bring quick results whether they are positive or negative. Make this very focused on a few promotions as this is a powerful team; when they are tasked with making the direct phone calls to get a decision, then they normally get one. When the decision is positive from the end user, then the revenue for that particular program takes off. When they are not, then more work must be done within the manufacturing or channel company. This could be a quick fix or a long-term change in some aspect of the product/promotion. If the fix is long-term, then take the program off the list and reapply later on. I again see no more than thirty-day programs on this promotion sheet and keep them manageable. The key is to have a strong inside sales manager to make sure results meet company expectations while making sure their team is not overloaded. Continue to strive for reduction in non-preselling work from this team. Also, continue to resist using this team as telemarketers. You should assign highly qualified people to this group working on programs that at times are sophisticated, require relationships and experience with current customers and channels.

With all this established, you will have the process built to evaluate the productivity of your sales team in the main area of growing the business and doing it quickly. Within a short period of time, you will begin to see programs either move forward or realize something needs to be done to get it right. You will also see where your sales team is falling short on customer and channel management. You will get the clear picture on just how customers are being managed and to what extent are they supporting your products. There is no hiding from the opportunity list, and everyone must participate. Now, it will become easy to see a territory picture and to then understand who the top salespeople are. Rather than just speculate on why a product line is or is not selling, this will also become clear. No longer can someone just make a statement or excuse about a shortfall in a new product selling. If a large percent of the sales team is having success, then you can dig into why a few are struggling. Likewise, if a large percent of the sales team is struggling, then you can find out what is wrong with the offering. Sales management can attend monthly top management meeting to verify the programs they have the sales team chasing are in line with the overall plan. It will be very easy to get a snapshot of current opportunities and report projected orders over a short period of time while also defining the sales stage they are implementing. This will give others an opportunity to offer assistance from a high level. I found that when you can get the high-level management involved with a few customer/channel opportunities, things generally move in a positive direction as they are happy to help. Everyone loves to be associated with assisting in getting orders.

Now, the stage is set as a company team focused on assisting the sales group to bring in their orders. You will have been successful in creating an environment that, as I started out with:

"Just let 'em sell!"

www.ingramcontent.com/pod-product-compliance
Lightning Source LLC
Chambersburg PA
CBHW022103170526
45157CB00004B/1468